INGÉNU

Forthcoming in the series:

and many more . . .

Ingénue

Joanna McNaney Stein

BLOOMSBURY ACADEMIC
NEW YORK · LONDON · OXFORD · NEW DELHI · SYDNEY

BLOOMSBURY ACADEMIC
Bloomsbury Publishing Inc
1385 Broadway, New York, NY 10018, USA
50 Bedford Square, London, WC1B 3DP, UK
29 Earlsfort Terrace, Dublin 2, Ireland

BLOOMSBURY, BLOOMSBURY ACADEMIC and the Diana logo are
trademarks of Bloomsbury Publishing Plc

First published in the United States of America 2024

Copyright © Joanna McNaney Stein, 2024

For legal purposes the Acknowledgments on p. ix constitute an extension
of this copyright page.

Library of Congress Cataloging-in-Publication Data

Names: McNaney Stein, Joanna, author.
Title: Ingénue / Joanna McNaney Stein.
Description: [1st.] | New York : Bloomsbury Academic, 2023. | Series: 33 1/3 | Includes
bibliographical references. | Summary: "The story of the album that finally brought the
spirited, talented Canadian vocalist out and into the spotlight"—Provided by publisher.
Identifiers: LCCN 2023009961 (print) | LCCN 2023009962 (ebook) | 9781501389191
(paperback) | ISBN 9781501389207 (ebook) | ISBN 9781501389214 (pdf)
| ISBN 9781501389221 (ebook other)
Subjects: LCSH: lang, k. d., 1961- Ingénue. | lang, k. d., 1961- | Popular music—
Canada—1991-2000—History and criticism. | Lesbian musicians—Canada.
Classification: LCC ML420.L23598 M36 2023 (print) | LCC ML420.L23598 (ebook) |
DDC 782.42164092—dc23/eng/20230307
LC record available at https://lccn.loc.gov/2023009961
LC ebook record available at https://lccn.loc.gov/2023009962

ISBN: PB: 978-1-5013-8919-1
ePDF: 978-1-5013-8921-4
eBook: 978-1-5013-8920-7

Series: 33 1/3

Typeset by Deanta Global Publishing Services, Chennai, India
Printed and bound in Great Britain

To find out more about our authors and books visit www.bloomsbury.com and sign up
for our newsletters.

To Beth, for the crazed, closeted teenagers we were.

Contents

CONTENTS

Acknowledgments

My deep gratitude to Leah Babb-Rosenfeld, Editor of Music and Sound Studies at Bloomsbury, for supporting this project, and to Sarah Piña for your fine-tuning and encouragement.

Thank you to the supremely talented Ben Mink, for your kindness, and to Josh Lattanzi, Fred Eltringham, Daniel Clarke, David Piltch, and Laura Veirs.

My never-ending thanks to Margot Stein for believing in me, and to our sweet, hilarious daughter Nina for drawing me pictures while I sat at the computer typing.

Endless appreciation to my friends and support network: Beth Abel, Kensey Lamb, Heather Moran, Evan Harrington, Kathryn Mahoney, Michael Cirino, Jill Bell, Matt Dorfman, April Ayers Lawson, Melissa Presti, Sara Traficante, Sam Bell, Dan McCarthy, Allie Langerak, Karen Niles, Jenn Oliveri, Brian Katz, Jessica Phillips-Lorenz, Griffin Hansbury, and Susannah Hyland.

Thank you to my family.

And lastly, to my colleagues at the City University of New York, Kingsborough, and to the editors at *Bust Magazine*, *PopMatters*, *The Brooklyn Rail*, and *The Hard Times*, thank you for your support.

Introduction

As a songwriter, singer, and performer, k.d. lang's interpretations of love, loss, and longing on her 1992 album *Ingénue* earned her critical acclaim and lifelong fans in the queer community and beyond. *Ingénue*, about lang's experience with unrequited love, gives listeners a chance to bear witness to the artist's vulnerability just as stardom was about to strike. Beyond lang's swift and sudden embrace by 1990s pop culture and the whirlwind of press that went along with publicly coming out, she is an artist who has broken boundaries of gender and genre.

In 1987, five years prior to *Ingénue*'s release, chief popular music critic Jon Pareles of *The New York Times* reviewed k.d. lang's live show at the Bottom Line in Greenwich Village: "K.D. Lang comes on strong" was his introductory sentence. A paragraph later, Pareles uses the word "Ingénue" to describe one of the many vocal personas lang transforms into while on stage.[1]

[1]Pareles, Jon. "CABARET: K.D. LANG, COUNTRY." *The New York Times*. May 10, 1987. https://www.nytimes.com/1987/05/10/arts/cabaret-kd-lang-country.html.

Whether the album title is, in any way, connected, I don't know, but it seemed a serendipitous sign.

Almost any work about a female musician is critical reading, so a book about a queer musician feels even more so. In the *Journal of Homosexuality*, Suzanne McLaren asserts, "Lack of a sense of belonging to the general community has been found as a predictor for depression in lesbians."[2] My hope is that this book fosters a sense of connectedness and belonging, particularly for LGBTQ+ readers and music fans (heavy emphasis on the *L*). However, *any* lover of well-composed pop music or folks wishing to broaden their scope of groundbreaking artists may also benefit from reading.

As a self-identified lesbian and a person who began the coming out process as a teenager at roughly the same time as *Ingénue*'s release, I weave in short personal anecdotes that connect to my experience of lang's work. Those sections are roped off with three asterisks (***). While I've debated whether or not these would hold any relevance for the reader, ultimately I've decided to let them speak for themselves.

As such, this hybrid genre book fits somewhat coincidentally into three parts: 33⅓ k.d. lang biography, 33⅓ memoir, and 33⅓ album review and analysis. Part I is a "pre-*Ingénue* primer," showcasing k.d. lang's rise to fame in her early "cowpunk" days with her band, the Reclines. Part II, more or less, sticks to the *Ingénue* album itself—including track-by-track analysis, behind-the-scenes

[2]McLaren, Suzanne. "Sense of Belonging to the General and Lesbian Communities as Predictors of Depression among Lesbians." *Journal of Homosexuality*, vol. 56, no. 1, January 2009, pp. 1–13.

information about the songwriting and recording process, and the manic media attention that unfolded in the immediate aftermath. Part III discusses *Ingénue*'s and k.d.'s prevailing legacy in contemporary pop culture. It also includes interviews with lang's musical collaborators: *Ingénue* writing partner/producer, Ben Mink, singer-songwriter Laura Veirs, drummer Fred Eltringham, and k.d.'s go-to pianist since *Watershed* (2008), Daniel Clarke.

My approach to writing goes beyond me, as a fan, enjoying k.d. lang's music because of our shared sexuality—though, as lang was officially coming out in *The Advocate* in 1992, I was coming out at home. The brilliant musicality of *Ingénue*, coupled with lang's bravery, left a lasting impression. It is my great privilege to write about lang's multifaceted artistry— as an avant-garde performer, singer, and activist—but, most importantly, to share my analysis of k.d. lang's *Ingénue*.

Part I
Pre-*Ingénue* Primer

When I met k.d. for the first time, she was wearing a cowboy shirt with these little figurines sewn on. I said, "Hey, hold on a second!" I went to the dressing room, and I had some of the same figurines glued to the inside of my violin. She couldn't believe it. I immediately got what she was trying to do. . . . And she had a God-given voice that doesn't come along more than a few times in a century.

—*Ben Mink**

*Mink, Ben. Personal Interview. Conducted by Joanna M. Stein. December 3, 2021.

1
k.d. lang's American TV Debut

The first time I watched the uninhibited, androgynous k.d. lang was her American TV debut on David Letterman's *Late Show* in 1986. I was ten years old. Luckily, my parents were huge Letterman fans, and they set the VCR to record his show on a nightly basis.

Letterman introduced k.d. as a "unique performer from Canada in her American television debut," and she bounced onto the stage enthusiastically like a punk Elvis in a cowgirl dress. With her band, the Reclines, she performed "Turn Me Round" off the then-forthcoming *Angel with a Lariat* album.

k.d. was ambiguously female and yet unapologetically masculine, all wrapped into one. I did not know that this identity was even a possibility yet. The concept of identifying as nonbinary or anything else wasn't in the cultural consciousness yet and certainly not in my consciousness. I was raised Catholic, so I had only conceived of girl/boy and male/female at that point. I vaguely knew that gay people existed, but I wasn't able to make that leap in my mind yet. Watching her perform back then, I was stunned into confusion and awe. Synapses that had not yet been connected in my brain fired wildly.

In a short interview following lang's performance, a baffled Letterman asks, "What kind of music was that? What would you call that?"

"I call that 'Torch and Twang' music," k.d. answers assuredly, "Torch music and Twang—good ol' Country and Western."

In *Engendered Charisma: k.d. lang and the Comic Frame*, Tracy Whalen writes, "The joy generated by lang's charismatic or 'pleasure-bearing' performances is kinetically instantiated in her early years, lang jumps, dances, curtsies, twirls, yodels, howls, chokes on lyrics, and hams it up." Whalen continues, "Gay and lesbian bodies, not to mention butch bodies, were strikingly absent in popular culture."[1] Even with increased homophobia during the height of the AIDS epidemic, lang fearlessly took to the American stage without a hint of self-consciousness.

According to Simon Frith, author of *Performance Rites: On the Value of Popular Music*, he writes "to perform for the audience as a woman means something different than to perform for the audience as a man . . . a woman's problem is how to keep control of herself in a space the stage patrolled by an objectifying [patriarchal] and sexual gaze. . . . The female performer is inevitably much more self-conscious than a male performer."[2]

---

[1] Whalen, Tracy. "Engendering Charisma: k.d. lang and the Comic Frame." *Intertexts*, vol. 18, no. 1, spring 2014, pp. 9+.

[2] Frith, Simon. *Performing Rites: On the Value of Popular Music*. Cambridge, MA: Harvard University Press, 1998.

In no way did lang embody the hetero-normative viewpoint that Frith describes of the self-conscious female performer. lang gave herself permission to relinquish all control, to be authentically who she wanted to be on stage without a second thought. Free from the shackles of prescribed gender expression, she performed with wild abandon.

Back home in Canada, with the Reclines, or "the boys," as lang liked to call them, k.d. already had a devoted following after her 1984 debut album, *A Truly Western Experience*. The cover of the first album looks not unlike a children's book: with collaged pictures of the sun and a barn, and Patsy Cline's face in one of the barn's windows. k.d. lang is dancing atop a nearby fence. This was a far cry from the lang that would emerge eight years later.

Shortly before her Letterman debut, 24-year-old k.d. lang sat down with journalist Jack Webster in 1985 for his *Webster!* Canadian talk show. With cropped hair, cat-eye glasses frames without lenses, and an embroidered satin Western shirt and bolo tie, k.d. lang is introduced as the "hottest thing in punk country." k.d. admits to having chopped off all her hair recently and shows off her sawed-off cowboy boots with a hole in the sole. Unable to resist, Webster immediately begins teasing her about her appearance:

WEBSTER. You are bizarre.
LANG. Thank you.
WEBSTER. I love your boots. Tell me about your boots
    . . .
LANG. They were given to me by a Polish farmer . . . in
    Consort, Alberta . . .

WEBSTER. There's no glass in your glasses!
LANG. They're psychic lenses, Jack.

The banter between them shows that k.d. could laugh at her quirkiness and that criticism rolled off her back without much thought. The tone of the interview changes, however, after Webster requests that k.d. play a song.

She picks up a black Takamine acoustic guitar, which she's likely borrowed from her bandmate, Ben Mink. As she strums, she notices the guitar is out of tune, but she says, "that's good." She's written a song about the legendary Patsy Cline, the person k.d. claimed to be the reincarnation of at the time, and the impetus for her band name, the "Re-clines." Her voice is clear, her vibrato is gorgeous, and suddenly the out-of-tune guitar becomes an afterthought. After she finishes, the entire production crew behind Webster breaks into cheers and applause.[3]

Critics would later describe k.d.'s image and music at this time as "country punk" or "cowpunk." Robin Elliott, in his article "Performing k.d. lang," described lang's "cowpunk" image as "both her *appearance*—spiky hair, retro glasses (with no lenses), sawn-off cowboy boots, etc.—and her *onstage antics as a performer*, which were manic and mischievous."[4]

[3]"Webster! Interview with K.D. lang." *YouTube*, uploaded by Royal BC Museum. October 24, 2014. https://www.youtube.com/watch?v=S_7ExsNi9pw.

[4]Elliott, Robin. "Performing k.d. lang." *Canadian Woman Studies*, vol. 24, no. 2–3, winter–spring 2005, pp. 120+.

On the podcast *Homo Sapiens*, hosted by Christopher Sweeney, lang discusses her background in performance art: "I had a lot of fun with the clothes: cut-off cowboy boots, ripped stockings, second-hand clothes, clothes made out of curtains. I came from the performance art perspective . . . it was really that I had a look that juxtaposed with the music. I loved to play with opposing ideas."[5]

In "Queer Thoughts: On Country Music and k.d. lang," Martha Mockus writes, "I was fascinated not only by the power, range, and depth of her voice but by the wonderful mixture of passion and mischief in her singing . . . the tight and playful sound of her band, the [R]eclines. Country music—in the hands of lang—could be fun after all." [6]

*   *   *

About a year later, lying awake in bed one night, I reached under my t-shirt and felt small lumps. I panicked; I had heard all about cancer. My mother's father died of leukemia, and my mom would eventually also die of cancer in 2012. But that night, my parents were up late watching TV when I came down the stairs. I yanked my mom away.

"Mom, I think I have tumors."
"What? What do you mean, honey?"

---

[5]Spirit Studios and Christopher Sweeney. "k.d. lang Part 1." *Homo Sapiens*, Spotify. August 2021.

[6]Mockus, Martha. "Queer Thoughts: On Country Music and k.d. lang." *Queering the Pitch*, ed. by Philip Brett, Elizabeth Wood, and Gary C. Thomas. Routledge, 1994, 349.

"I mean, cancer, maybe."

"Joanna, what are you talking about?"

"Up here and here, on my chest. I feel something!"

I can't remember if my mother laughed or not, but she said, "Joanna, you're getting breasts, honey, go back to sleep." I walked back up the stairs, destroyed. Breasts, I thought at the time, would surely be worse than cancer.

A few months later, outdated films in health class explained the process of growing breasts was called "development," a term that was familiar to me only in the context of signs left by construction companies on empty dirt lots. I imagined tiny families in little plastic houses popping on my chest like *Monopoly*.

Around the same time, I started locking myself in the bathroom at home, splashing water from the faucet into my hair, and then slicking it back with a comb. *Not bad*, I thought. I frequently remembered lang's *Letterman* performance, so I gave myself some permission to explore.

One time, I bravely stepped out of the bathroom to show my younger brother. In addition to my *Grease Lightnin'* hairstyle this time, I'd even zipped my brother's too-tight bomber jacket over my new developments. My brother fell over with laughter when he saw me, then called my older sister down from our shared bedroom to check me out. When I heard my siblings' laughter, not knowing what else to do, I turned it all into a practical joke.

My sister handed me a pair of my father's sunglasses that were sitting on top of his dresser to complete the look. My brother snapped a picture. I am standing with my sister in my parents' bedroom in the photo. My sister is squinting and making a little kissy face as if she were my fangirl.

As always, when I was anxious, I tried to be funny. We made many prank phone calls as kids, inspired by the Jerky Boys, no doubt, and since we had an exciting new speakerphone, now we could all listen in.

I took the opportunity to initiate a call to our neighbor girl across the street.

"Tell her I'm a boy—your cousin visiting from another country," I said as I handed Adam the phone. "I'll lower my voice."

I was desperate to feel how a girl would respond if she thought I were a boy (even if it were just over the phone and the neighbor girl was only half buying it). I also enjoyed keeping on the outfit long after the phone call ended.

Though I wasn't going for a k.d.-inspired country-punk look back then, I was going for something. Many times during puberty, I imagined myself as the charming leading man in an old black-and-white movie—the kind of character who removes his trench coat to drape it over a puddle for his girlfriend to walk over. Up to that point, all the misguided fantasies I had about gender roles and relationships were fueled by those antiquated images. Then along came k.d. lang on TV, moving from a place of authenticity like I'd never seen before.

*   *   *

Ben Mink, cowriter/coproducer of *Ingénue* and lang's longtime musical collaborator, didn't join the Reclines until their second album, *Angel with a Lariat* (1985). His songwriting abilities and musical contributions to the band as a multi-instrumentalist (guitar, mandolin, violin) would become invaluable.

When I interviewed Mink, we discussed the *Letterman* debut. I described to him how thrilling it was to watch as a child. Mink tells me—with genuine Canadian kindness—he's glad to hear it:

> It's great to hear a memory, to know it sticks with someone like you. You know, we just do it. You don't know who you'll reach or how . . . I don't think I was ever more nervous than that night [Letterman]. In the video, I can see myself hyper-ventilating.[7]

While Mink was filled with anxiety joining the Reclines for their American TV debut, lang's anxiety—if there was any—was channeled through her wild physicality. Critics like Mockus and Elliott both agree that lang's early performances were "mischievous," and even though I wasn't certain who I wanted to be in the world yet, watching lang's mischief-making on stage helped me develop a playful, and less painful, experience of sexuality.

---

[7]Mink, Ben. Personal Interview. Conducted by Joanna M. Stein. December 3, 2021.

2
In Search of a Missing Identity

* * *

My mother almost named me Caroline after the 1969 Neil Diamond hit, "Sweet Caroline." Even though I have a soft spot for Neil, this would have been a critical error. Caroline would have been a completely different person. Caroline would have been far more reserved, conservative even. Caroline would be the CEO of an advertising firm, wear pantsuits and own an assortment of brown leather purses.

Caroline would be, most definitely, straight.

So instead I was named Joanna after the lead character in the "feminist horror," *The Stepford Wives*.[1] The plot of the 1975 movie, based on the novel by Ira Levin, centers on the character Joanna Eberhart, who moves to the fictional town of Stepford, Connecticut, with her husband, after which she

---

[1] Arrow, Michelle. "'Suburban Living Did Turn Women into Robots': Why Feminist Horror Novel *The Stepford Wives* Is Still Relevant 50 Years On." *The Conversation*. July 25, 2022.

promptly loses her identity and transforms into a submissive, robotic housewife.

I spent a good part of the 1980s hunting for my name on kitschy merchandise. I envied kids whose names were on personalized pencils, balloons and mini-license plates: *Jessica, Jill, Joan . . . Joanne . . .* so close. At a music store, I finally found the 45 rpm single of Kool & the Gang's "Joanna" off their 1983 album *In the Heart*. The song made me cringe, especially since friends in elementary school had started serenading me with it, but since a 45 was only a few bucks back then, my mom bought it for me.

Around the same time, friends at school were starting to whisper about sex. I had no idea what it meant, but I wanted to know. Once, while tearing apart the edges of my golden Styrofoam tray during lunch at elementary school, I asked a friend.

"What's sex?"

"Well I can't tell you!" she said, shocked.

"Why not? What's the big deal? What is sex? WHAT IS SEX?"

The whole lunch table burst into screamy kid laughter. I was going to have to do my own research.

The first explanation to my sex question would be answered in the form of a comically outdated four-book collection called *The Life Cycle Library* (1969). Literally not knowing any better at the time, I plotted to steal one of the books from my father's bookcase.

When my parents had gone out one day, I approached the bookcase like I was a character planning a heist from *Ocean's Eleven*. To make matters worse, my dad's bookcase was an antique with sliding glass covers for each of the shelves. Miscellaneous doodads and heirlooms were laid out along the top of it: my dead great-grandfather's black fedora that I liked to wear from time to time, a brown bakelite shortwave radio, and a good half dozen of my mother's decorative paperweights. I opened it quietly so my siblings wouldn't catch on, grabbed one book, tucked it under my arm, and ran like hell to my bedroom. I kept the book hidden far under my bed for years.

When my mom finally gave me "the sex talk" it was the Roman Catholic version. She sat down on the front steps of our small porch in the burbs and told me, "When a man and a woman love each other, they get married, and when they want to be close to each other and have a baby, they have sex."

"But what *is it*?" I asked.

"Well, men have penises, and women have vaginas. The man's penis goes inside the woman's vagina and that is what sex is." There were absolutely, positively no alternative explanations given.

After completing several angry and awkward cartwheels in the grass, I staged a protest, stomping and shouting, "I'm never having sex! I'm never having sex! I'm never having sex!"

Later, as a teen, I would visit Barnes and Noble searching for literary proof that someone like me even existed. Lesbian writing, if any, was usually miscategorized under the umbrella of "women's studies" or "sociology" on the second floor. My hands would become clammy holding the black rubber handrail of the escalator as I went up. Once I got to "women's studies", I would nervously scan titles while keeping a lookout for anyone who might see me. Since I couldn't find hope on the shelves and was on the verge of a panic attack, I ditched the bookstore for the movie theater.

A faint glimmer of hope shined down when *Fried Green Tomatoes* was released in 1991. Adapted from Fannie Flagg's 1987 novel, the movie starred Mary-Louise Parker and Mary Stuart Masterson. While Parker and Masterson did their best as Ruth and Idgie to act out the sexual tension in the subtext, the script simmered down Flagg's original lesbian characterization to a cozy friendship.

Before that time, Alice Walker's 1982 devastatingly beautiful novel *The Color Purple* had also been adapted into a 1985 film. However, the film also cut out most of the lesbian content. Instead it was reduced to a kiss between characters Celie (played by real-life lesbian Whoopi Goldberg) and Shug (played by Margaret Avery).

Most queer movies that followed in the next few years were primarily thrillers. LGBTQ+ characters were either homicidal, suicidal, or both. With the real threat of HIV and AIDS looming in the air, it's no wonder that sex and death were so intertwined.

I sneaked into the movie theater to see Paul Verhoven's psycho-sexual thriller *Basic Instinct* in 1992. Sharon Stone played Catherine Trammel, a hot bisexual psychopath, and her lover Roxy (Leilani Sarelle) was also a hot bisexual psychopath. After savoring a brief kiss in one scene, Catherine rests her hand on Roxy's breast. A woman touching another woman's breast was shocking (and also awesome). Later, Roxy becomes so enraged at Catherine's new male lover Nick (Michael Douglas) that she stalks him, then tries to mow him down in her car. Failing to kill him, a suspenseful car chase ensues, and she accidentally drives herself off a cliff. Another one bites the dust.

Peter Jackson's biographical thriller *Heavenly Creatures* (1994), which was Kate Winslet and Melanie Lynskey's film debut, depicted a more realistic relationship, but as it was chillingly revealed on screen, the two teenage lovers commit matricide. To make matters worse, the film was based on the real-life 1954 Parker-Hulme murder case. Forget about glimmers of hope. If bookstores couldn't help, and movie theaters couldn't help, maybe the record shop could.

*　*　*

If I thought signs of queer identity were hard to come by in the early 1990s in a suburb of Rochester, New York, with a population of around 25,000 at the time, it was certainly more difficult to find it in the Prairies of Canada in the 1970s. lang's hometown of Consort, Alberta, had roughly a population of 600.

In *Rolling Stone*, Keltie lang, one of k.d.'s older siblings (k.d. is the youngest of four children), was interviewed along with k.d. with whom she lived at the time. Keltie describes k.d. as a "rambunctious tomboy" growing up, who came out "when she was just a young teenager" in Consort. "It wasn't some hideous trashy lesbian pulp novel from the 50s. She wasn't, like, tortured about it."

Though her sibling's recollections of k.d.'s coming out were free of dramatic twists and turns, it wasn't without loss; their father left the family when k.d. was only twelve. In *Rolling Stone* she admits, "I was really very close to him before he left."[2] In other interviews, she touched upon her suspicion that her father may have been closeted. "My father—who has now passed away—was probably a bit gay, and a great singer."[3]

Discussing her family and coming out on the *Homo Sapiens* podcast, lang stated, "I had a very supportive family. Three out of four children are gay, but I'm the youngest and was the first one out. . . . It was 1979 . . . that was pretty early in the Prairies." Thankfully, lang's sexuality was embraced by her family, and when she needed to feel part of a community, she headed to the clubs. One can imagine a young k.d. revved up and ready to go out for the night, maybe with a swagger a bit like John Travolta's character in *Saturday Night Fever*.

"I spent most of my youth in gay clubs before I even started my career . . . I mean [now] there's Tinder, and there's instant gratification, but there's not [the] figure out your outfit, and call your friends, and go out for dinner, and go home and have a nap, and get ready to go."[4]

During the time of her early TV performances, lang may not have still been going to clubs regularly, but she was undoubtedly "ready to go." Later, she would merge her vocal abilities with her bravado to become a star.

[2]lang as qtd. in Udovitch. "k.d. lang." *Rolling Stone.* August 5, 1993, 55–7.

[3]Philby, Charlotte. "My Secret Life: KD Lang." *The Independent.* July 25, 2009. https://www.independent.co.uk/news/people/profiles/my-secret-life -kd-lang-1757220.html.

[4]lang as qtd. on Podcast. "k.d. lang Part 1." *Homo Sapiens*, Spotify. August 2021.

3
The Tonight Show, Patsy Cline, and "Crying"

After *Letterman*, k.d. was invited to perform on *The Tonight Show* with Johnny Carson. For her 1987 debut, she covered Patsy Cline's "In Care of the Blues," which was also recorded for the Reclines' second album, *Angel with a Lariat*. lang's collegiate background in performance art was on full display on stage, as she dropped to her knees during the song's final moments wailing away. Carson was transfixed.

When Carson saw talent, he kept it close; just one week later, k.d. was invited back to *The Tonight Show*. For her second Carson appearance, she sang two songs, "Turn Me Round," which she'd performed on *Letterman*, and another Cline ballad "Three Cigarettes (in an Ashtray)." For "Cigarettes," lang performs while sitting at a table set literally with three cigarettes in an ashtray. Under the spotlight, lang performs like an actor in a one-act play, with pained facial expressions, a vein in her neck throbbing, and her trembling hand reaching out as she sustains the final note.

When the camera cuts to Carson's reaction, he is wiping a tear away from his eye and saying, "That's marvelous. She can sing, can't she? She is a real, pure singer."[1] Enamored, Carson had her back several more times to perform songs off of 1989's Grammy Award-winning album *Absolute Torch and Twang* and *Shadowlands* (1988), which she recorded with Patsy Cline's former producer, Owen Bradley.

During these vintage televised performances, it's clear—from the fringed dresses she wore to the vocal scoops—that she was imitating Cline, though lang would later differentiate herself:

> I became absolutely obsessed with Patsy Cline. I started getting all these inspirational visions of how I could play with country music—play with the clothes . . . the structure . . . the themes . . . I was around a lot of punk musicians and people at the time. I started thinking, "Let's mix punk and country" and created k.d. lang and the Reclines.[2]

In many early interviews, lang discussed her firm belief that she was the reincarnation of Patsy Cline. The guitar strap k.d. wore in her younger days was even decorated with "K.D. LANG" in custom chain stitching down the front, and "PATSY CLINE LIVES" at the bottom. Perhaps lang's

---

[1]"Turn Me Round and 3 Cigarettes k.d. lang Back on Carson Show a Week Later!" *YouTube*, uploaded by Declan John. n.d. https://www.youtube.com/watch?v=BD_n6ju9iRA.

[2]Spirit Studios and Christopher Sweeney. "k.d. lang Part 1." *Homo Sapiens*, Spotify. August 2021.

insistence on Cline's soul continuing on after death actually foreshadowed lang's future life as a Buddhist.[3]

In many ways, lang is the superior performer. I understand if readers want to throw this book in the trash now. Before you do, hear me out. Patsy Cline was fierce and feisty and fought for what she wanted as an artist long before it was acceptable to do so. Cline's vocal charm and singing abilities were unquestionably there, but lang's vocal tone is deeper, warmer, and more inviting. As a performer, lang blew the lid off of Cline. Certainly, women were restricted by societal and cultural rules, whether implicit or explicit, in Cline's era—in which case, it's fair to assume that those boundaries prevented Cline from trying such daring stunts as lang in the mid-1980s.

Cline talk aside, by 1989, lang's fearlessness paid off in the North American country music market, and the accolades started rolling in. She took home two Grammy awards that year, one for Best Country Female Vocal Performance for her album *Absolute Torch and Twang* and Best Country Collaboration for "Crying," her duet with the legendary Roy Orbison.[4]

Even though Orbison had originally released "Crying" in 1961, and the song was previously covered by Don McLean in 1980, the lang/Orbison version held a power like no other. Before Orbison's death in 1988, the two performed the song

---

[3]For some critics, the reincarnation claim didn't make sense as Cline died two after lang was born.

[4]The duet was featured on the soundtrack of the 1987 film *Hiding Out*.

together live on both *The Tonight Show* and BBC's *Top of the Pops.*

At this time, perhaps due to the new attention, lang also began to refine her early cowpunk image to a more mainstream persona. She began performing in suits instead of cowboy boots but still "retained [her] alternative edge" and controversial androgynous appearance.

In a 1992 interview with Bob Costas, lang talks about how pivotal working with Orbison was for her:

> Roy's influence in my life, beyond musically, has been immense. He was very powerful, and very strong, and very quiet and Zen-like—like a tree. Peaceful, very strong, and very still. We were both very tentative about doing "Crying" as a duet, because it's more of a solo, but it worked. . . . It was a real joy to sing with Roy.[5]

Whalen writes, "Like the androgynous lang, Orbison resists legibility; his voice and body convey a quiet vulnerability that contradicts conventional masculine codes." With Orbison the bravado that is combine seen in a male performer is strikingly absent.

"Orbison has a tremulous voice, an operatic vocal style, and occasional falsetto—all musical markers of queerness," Whalen continues. While a "tremulous voice" is not necessarily a "marker of queerness," Orbison is an almost incomparable performer unless one compares him to lang.

---

[5] "k. d. lang Interview on Sexuality Patsy Cline and Roy Orbison—Later with Bob Costas 4/28/92." *YouTube*, uploaded by clevelandlivemusic. February 16, 2021. https://www.youtube.com/watch?v=1LW4p7GLof8.

Orbison, like lang, was an outlier in pop music. His looks and his sound were unconventional for a pop singer in the 1950s and 1960s. He wore dark sunglasses, which sometimes led audiences to believe he was blind; instead, it was because Orbison suffered from stage fright.[6] He did not fit into prescribed characteristics of masculinity, as lang does not assume conventional feminine roles. When performing together, an opposite expectation occurs: Orbison is reserved and quiet, stereotypical trademarks of femininity, while lang moves deliberately and boisterously, mannerisms that are seen as stereotypically masculine.[7]

In 2004, lang wrote a short article about her "kinship" with Orbison for *Rolling Stone*'s "The Immortals—Greatest Artists of All Time" list:

> We were rehearsing the song in the studio . . . and Roy and I happened to be sharing a mic. When we got to a part where we were singing at the same time, we both leaned into the mic and our cheeks touched. His cheek was so soft, and the energy was so amazing. Not sexual but totally explosive, like the chemistry of some sort of kinship. I'll never forget what that felt like.[8]

[6]"Roy Orbison." *Memphis Music Hall of Fame.* https://memphismusichal loffame.com/inductee/royorbison/.

[7]Whalen, Tracy. "Engendering Charisma: k.d. lang and the Comic Frame." *Intertexts*, vol. 18, no. 1, spring 2014, pp. 9+.

[8]lang, k.d. "The Immortals—Greatest Artists of All Time: 37—Roy Orbison." *Rolling Stone,* no. 946. April 15, 2004.

4
Torch and Twang Days

On k.d. lang and the Reclines' third album *Absolute Torch and Twang* (1989), stand-out tracks like "Trail of Broken Hearts" and "Pullin' Back the Reins" were torch ballads cowritten by lang and Mink. "Big Big Love" was another, more upbeat highlight, a cover of a 1960s country two-step jam that harkened back to her earlier country days.

As stated in Frith, the torch song is an

> elegy to unrequited love . . . is the clearest example of the pop singer's interpretive art. . . . Although torch singers presented particular feelings describing particular situations (romantic illusions and disillusion) our pleasure in the song lies not in the drama of the event, but in the way the singers explore the nuances of feeling.[1]

lang said, "[T]he reason I chose the words 'torch' and 'twang' is that I would love to marry ballad-jazz and country. Those

[1]Frith, Simon. *Performing Rites: On the Value of Popular Music*. Cambridge, MA: Harvard University Press, 1998.

are the types of music I'm most passionate about. People have incorporated jazz into country [music] before, but I don't think anyone's dedicated their life to it."[2]

Only two singles from *Torch and Twang* were released for airplay, "Full Moon Full of Love" and "Three Days." Both were overlooked. Warner Brothers even produced an official music video for "Trail of Broken Hearts," which only charted at 87 on the top 100 on the Canadian charts. "Pullin' Back the Reins" was later released as another single but failed to make the charts in North America.

Despite her obvious vocal talent and winning a Grammy for the album, country music stations excluded her from their playlists. Though k.d. was not hiding anything, rumors about her sexuality circulated widely. The obstacles she faced had nothing to do with her music and everything to do with her perceived sexuality and gender presentation.

In "Performing k.d. lang," Elliot discusses gender presentation on the album cover of *Torch and Twang*: "she posed in the middle of a wheat field with cowboy hat in hand: a traditional 'country' image. . . . But the short hair, together with her generally androgynous physical appearance and outfit, made her look more like a cowboy in drag rather than a cowgirl."[3]

[2]lang as qtd. in Mockus. "Queer Thoughts: On Country Music and k.d. lang." *Queering the Pitch*, ed. by Philip Brett, Elizabeth Wood, and Gary C. Thomas. Routledge, 1994, 353.

[3]Elliott, Robin. "Performing k.d. lang." *Canadian Woman Studies*, vol. 24, no. 2–3, winter–spring 2005, pp. 160+.

Elliot's "cowboy in drag" point, diminishes k.d.'s butch identity. Viewing the cover as a gay woman, lang's butchness is on display, rather than the idea of her looking like a man dressing as a woman. This obviously comes later in *Ingénue* when she embodies "Miss Chatelaine." The *Torch and Twang* album cover may have caused confusion in some fans, nevertheless, lang moved further from "cowpunk" to the more earnest "cowboy" image.

Larry Wanagas, lang's first manager, said in *Billboard* magazine, "She just had a bit of a rough time with some of the country community and they had a rough time with her. I think country radio thought she was making fun of them, but she never had a problem with the fans or with the press or with television."[4]

The idea of what Wanagas calls k.d.'s "rough time" was most certainly due to those in the country "community." Since lang didn't fit the traditional country mold even remotely—that is, a straight woman with "the higher the hair, the closer to God" coiffure and philosophy—the country stations responded by omitting her from the airwaves. *Torch and Twang* didn't get nearly the kind of exposure that it deserved.

On *Homo Sapiens* podcast, lang reflects on this time in her life. "I was definitely loving the fact that I was different, and I was brazen. I was busting down doors, and smashing ceilings, and I loved that. I especially loved it in country music." Luckily, those deciding who would win

---

[4]Wanagas as qtd. in Newman. Newman, Melinda. "Grammy Win Propels lang to Platinum Status." *Billboard*, vol. 105, no. 12, March 20, 1993, pp. 1+.

a Grammy in 1989 listened to her voice, instead of simply judging her based on her perceived sexuality and gender presentation.

Years later, in *Vanity Fair*, where she famously posed with Cindy Crawford for the iconic cover, which will be discussed in a later chapter, lang clarified, "They [the country stations] were afraid of offending their listeners and losing advertisers."[5] She knew in order to gain acceptance from the country crowd, she would need to compromise her own butchness. Thankfully, compromise was not part of lang's vocabulary.

In between *Torch and Twang* and *Ingénue*, lang covered Cole Porter's classic "So in Love" for a 1990 benefit album for HIV/AIDS awareness called *Red Hot+Blue*. Not only did lang's work on the compilation display her commitment as an activist, her "smoky bossa nova" version of "So in Love," as *The New York Times* described it, became a musical bridge to *Ingénue*.[6]

As stated in *PopMatters*, "lang makes such warm liquid tones out of words like 'close' and 'strange' that we have a tactile sense of her nearness. She gets rich, wine-dark inflections out of her lower range, and then, during the chromatic ascent, her voice becomes seductively pliant."[7]

[5]Bennetts, Leslie. "k.d. lang Cuts It Close." *Vanity Fair*. August 1, 1993. https://www.vanityfair.com/style/1993/08/kd-lang-cover-story.

[6]Holden, Stephen. "POP VIEW; Why Cole Porter Prevails—Be It Pop, Rock, or Even Rap." *New York Times*. October 21, 1990.

[7]"Cole Porter in the Age of AIDS: The 25th Anniversary of 'Red Hot + Blue.'" *PopMatters*. November 19, 2015. https://www.popmatters.com

"So in Love" illustrated how lang's capabilities as a vocalist reached far beyond the country music market. To stay in country music's narrow, conservative world might have stymied her career entirely. Even though many times over her decades-long career, lang has stressed that sexuality was not what she wanted to sell her music. "Sexuality, yes, is a part of my music because it's a part of life. It's a basic need, but it's not how I want to be thought of. I'm an *artist*. That's what I want to talk about."[8] *Ingénue*, and her daring public declaration shortly thereafter, untethered lang from all previous expectations.

Up to this point, we've reminisced on lang's musical background, her gender and sexuality as it pertains to her stage persona, and how her time with the Reclines allowed her to push the boundaries of convention. Then along came *Ingénue* . . .

The album is a chameleon, and the response to the album changes with the listener. A literary listener, for instance, could hear the album as a queer autobiography of sorts, with lyrics that depict lang's desire to be loved and accepted. A music theorist might hear how the vocal melody of each song floats in and out of the chords. A sound engineer might hear how cleverly it was recorded, how the sometimes disparate parts come together to form the whole of each track. One thing that is undeniable about the album—the thing that

/cole-porter-in-the-age-of-aids-the-25th-anniversary-of-red-hot-blue -2495469079.html.

[8]Kohanov, Linda. "Chanteuse Extraordinaire: k.d. lang." *Pulse!*. April 1992, 73–7.

sustains it—is lang's vocal artistry. Whether or not lang wanted sexuality to sell the album, it certainly didn't hurt. In 1990s pop culture, perhaps, nowhere was the merging of sexuality and artistry perhaps more on display than with *Ingénue*.

Part II
Ingénue

5
Ben Mink on *Ingénue*

After *Torch and Twang*, Mink knew that he and lang were at an impasse with country music. Despite their great respect for the genre, Mink says they felt stuck because of "the whole gender issue." Unsure where to go next, both lang and Mink sat down to discuss what they could do.

"k.d. and I looked at each other and said, 'Well, what do you want to do?' She was listening to more jazz, but we didn't want to do a departure [from *Torch & Twang*] so drastic that every person would say, 'What in the world's going on here?' Beyond that, we just honestly sat down and said, 'Let's just have fun, it may be the last record we get a chance to do . . . then it took up every moment of our lives for at least a year. It was very, very involved."[1]

The son of Polish Holocaust survivors, Mink drew ideas from his family background to come up with the music for *Ingénue*. "I remember showing k.d. pictures of my family and

---

[1]Mink, Ben. Personal Interview. Conducted by the author. December 3, 2021.

my dad after the war. In post-war Germany, there was this whole rollicking Cabaret thing, which is always somehow mixed with depression and happiness at the same time. I started writing with that impression in mind."

Even though he and k.d. approached the songwriting from unrelated places, Mink from his family background and lang from her experience with unrequited love, they merged their melancholy ideas together to create *Ingénue*.

"['Constant Craving'] was originally called 'Easter Passover,' because we started writing it on a day when it was both Easter and Passover," recalled Mink in an interview for *Mix Online*. "We spent three days just on the chorus, because we couldn't decide exactly what notes to use. Sometimes songs come quickly, sometimes they take a while."[2] In total, Mink remembers, the album took roughly three months to write.

Mink recalls that many of the final vocal parts for lang were directly transferred from the original demos. *Ingénue* bassist David Piltch, who had played fretless on *Torch and Twang*'s "Pullin' Back the Reins" also remembers the demos. "The demos were already incredible by the time I got there. As I recall, Ben had been hard at work with k.d. doing a tremendous amount of pre-production. All I really had to do was listen to the music, contribute [to the] feel, and compliment the song."[3]

---

[2]Jackson, Blair. "Classic Track: 'Constant Craving,' k.d. lang." *Mix Magazine Online*. August 1, 2013.

[3]Piltch, David. "Re: Form Submission—Inquiries." Received by Joanna McNaney Stein. January 24, 2023. Email Interview.

Mink says, "We knew we had something special [with the demos], and we built around it. . . . Then Greg Penny came in as our co-producer, and we had a wonderful young engineer Marc Ramaer."

Penny had produced *Torch and Twang* before *Ingénue*, so they all knew how to work well together. He is also best known for his production work with Elton John, including the track "Teardrops" with lang from Elton's *Duets* album (1993).

In the spring of 1991, writing for *Ingénue* began. Mink recalls this time in his life as being particularly sweet. "It was 1991, and spring was in the air. It became this wonderful playground where we would get together and write every day. I was living in Toronto, but I was staying in Vancouver at the time. I even met my wife during that period, so there was a lot of change."

What began as a playground was later meticulously sculpted into the album that *Ingénue* became. Ramaer, who had assisted as an engineer on *Torch and Twang*, was available at Vancouver Studios, where the album was later recorded. Subsequent overdubs and mixing of vocals and instruments were done at Skip Saylor recording studio in Los Angeles.

"It was all coming from the right place, you know? It was a very honest, vulnerable record, and we weren't chasing anything except our own muse. . . . Every note was considered. If there was a sound we felt was too contemporary, which would date the piece as exactly 1992, we didn't use it," Mink asserted. "We wanted to use timeless elements, and a certain esoteric quality that would transcend all that and be timeless."

When the record execs flew into Vancouver to get a first listen to *Ingénue*, Mink said, they didn't appreciate any of it.

> Warner Brothers said, "We want to hear what you're doing." And, you know, they flew in, and we had even set up a room with flowers. Then, they just sat there—not understanding it. We were just heartbroken. A lot of the vocals were not done yet, but when it was finally finished, it was a whole different game. . . . It's amazing now to look back 30 years ago and see what we actually did, because I think it really holds up.[4]

What they didn't know at the time was not only would *Ingénue* take off, but it would also go platinum within a year of its release, and k.d. would soon win her third Grammy for Best Female Pop Vocal Performance.[5]

In agreement with Mink's earlier ideas about the album, lang called *Ingénue* a "post-nuclear cabaret." Appropriately, Mink recalls that German-born singer/actress Marlene Deitrich was a huge vocal influence for k.d. at the time. Potentially in homage to Deitrich, *Ingénue*'s cover art is reminiscent of *The Essential Marlene Dietrich*, a 1991 collection of Deitrich's work that came out while Mink and lang were cowriting songs for *Ingénue*.

Both album covers are in sepia tones, and the thin-lined font is even alike. The primary focus of the *Ingénue* cover is of lang gazing downward, and Deitrich was similarly posed.

---

[4]Mink, Ben. Personal Interview. Conducted by the author. December 3, 2021.

[5]By 1996, *Ingenue* went 2x multiplatinum in North America and Australia.

lang, with her hair still short, is parted and swept down instead of the familiar spikiness. She wears a white-collared shirt, unbuttoned at the top with the collar popped up. Gone was the lang from the child-like *Truly Western Experience* and the lone cowboy-hat-wearing lesbian in the wheat field from *Absolute Torch and Twang*. More subdued and pensive than ever before, k.d. lang and her *Ingénue* album were ready.

6
Ingénue Track-by-Track

Track 1. "Save Me"

For 1992, *Ingénue*'s sound was entirely unique—especially when contrasted with the commercial explosion of male-led rock, grunge, and hip-hop artists.[1] As always, lang's difference from the status quo was there, and her jazz and European influences were evident from the start.

The opening eight bars of *Ingénue* begin with the slow swinging "Save Me." The track features Mink alternating from G to Fmaj7 chords on his Takamine EF-series acoustic guitar and the warm upright bass of Toronto-native David Piltch, who as a teen played with trumpeter Chet Baker and saxophonist Art Pepper,[2] along with Greg Leisz weeping away on pedal steel.

---

[1] Def Leppard, Soundgarden, Primus, and Kris Kross also released albums in March 1992.

[2] "David Piltch." *The Canadian Encyclopedia.* May 9, 2007. https://www.the canadianencyclopedia.ca/en/article/david-piltch-emc.

Leisz's work on the track helps to bridge the genre gap between *Torch and Twang* and *Ingénue.* Also of note is vibraphonist Gary Burton—one of the first jazz musicians to publicly come out, shortly after lang in 1994[3]—who adds a dreamy new element to *Ingénue*, with his unique four-mallet vibraphone technique.

In a 1992 interview with *The Los Angeles Times*, lang discussed her jazz influences:

> I was listening to people like Julie London and Peggy Lee and Billie Holiday, and I found myself really being attracted to the strength in their subtleties. I tried not to use my power range at all on this record . . . on the country stuff I was relying on that . . . I wanted to explore the other areas of my voice, and use intensity not in volume, but in emotion.[4]

Despite its slow pace, at a tempo around 92 bpm, lang's vocal performance on "Save Me" is lush, emotional, and dynamic, and her leaps in her vocal range are highlighted throughout the verses. The slow tempo was a concern for lang, as mentioned in a 2017 interview with NPR:

> Ben [Mink] and I . . . were consciously aware of the fact that no one was making this kind of Eastern-European

---

[3]Burton, Gary. "Jazz Vibraphonist Gary Burton." *Fresh Air*, hosted by Terry Gross. *NPR*. January 5, 1994. https://freshairarchive.org/guests/gary-burton.
[4]Cromelin, Richard. "POP MUSIC: For k.d. Lang it's Bye-Bye, Patsy—Hello, *Ingénue.*" *Los Angeles Times.* August 2, 1992. https://www.latimes.com/archives/la-xpm-1992-08-02-ca-5557-story.html.

dirge . . . I thought that I would just get killed for [the tempo] being so slow. And I did. There was a lot of criticism on the record when it first came out.[5]

When lang's voice comes in for the first time, the phrasing is reminiscent of fellow Canadian Joni Mitchell's "Help Me" from her Grammy Award-winning album, *Court and Spark* (1974). Though Mitchell's song is more uptempo, and her voice entirely a different animal, lang vocally draws out the long "a" vowel sound in "save" is similar to Mitchell's short "e" sound of "help:"

> Saaaaaave me, Saaaaaave me from you/
> But paaaaaave me the waaaaay to you . . .

Throughout the introductory track, lang's voice also embodies what musicologist Elizabeth Wood describes as "Sapphonics" in the book *Queering the Pitch* (1994):

> I call Sapphonic this type of voice that refuses standard categories and is today considered a rare phenomenon. . . . The extreme range in one female voice . . . its defective break at crossing register borders produces an effect I call sonic cross-dressing: a merging rather than splitting of "butch" authority and "femme" ambiguity, an acceptance and integration of male and female.[6]

---

[5]Hilton, Robin. "k.d. lang Reflects on 25 Years of Ingénue." *NPR*. July 13, 2017.

[6]Wood, Elizabeth. "Sapphonics." *Queering the Pitch*, ed. by Philip Brett, Elizabeth Wood, and Gary C. Thomas. New York: Routledge, 1994, 51.

This "integration of male and female" can be heard in the song's lyrics:

> Lead me upon the captive free/
> Gracious and tame like love can be . . .

k.d. jumps from her lower vocal register as she sings, "lead me upon the . . ." into the higher "femme" head voice of "captive free . . ." and once again on the next line "gracious and tame like . . . love can be . . ." This vocal "merging" of the "butch" and "femme" occurs again with the lyrics "watch over me with a lover's eye / judging my worth only to glorify . . ." Even though it's doubtful that lang intended this, especially since the album predates the term "Sapphonics," the impact of lang's jumps in range at those moments is worth contemplating.

Track 2. "The Mind of Love"

Almost everyone has had the experience of talking to themselves. We might catch ourselves finishing one side of an argument to reach a more desirable conclusion, or maybe we simply say our own names aloud during moments of frustration. Other times we mutter to ourselves to gain a sense of control over something which feels out of control. The second track of *Ingénue*, "The Mind of Love" speaks to that turbulant feeling. It's the perfect metaphor for lang's experience with unrequited love that fuels the album.

"The Mind of Love," at a slightly increased tempo of 97 bpm, gives listeners the chance to hear k.d. refer to herself in the third person, not as "k.d." but as her given name "Kathryn," throughout the song. She starts the first verse with:

> Talking to myself here/
> is causing great concern for my health/
> Where is your head, Kathryn?/
> Where is your head?

Listeners know immediately that this is a conversation lang is having with herself, debating why she continues to pursue a woman who doesn't love her back. "I'm trying hard to escape this constant pull towards ache . . ." she goes on to sing.

At first listen, hearing lang refer to herself as the feminized "Kathryn" is both jarring and fascinating. It leads one to wonder whether the voices in her head that she discusses hearing are actually her own or mingled with echoes from her past.

Throughout the track, lang repeatedly asks herself rhetorical questions. Besides the first question "Where is your head, Kathryn?," she adds later, "Why do you fight, Kathryn?". This illustrates how critical lang is of her own behavior, which she describes in somewhat masochist terms as "the constant pull towards ache."

The final verse starts similarly to the first, with the addition of the word "again."

"I'm talking to myself *again*—it's causing great concern for my health." The "again" hints at lang's obsessiveness and allows listeners to hear how distressed she has become. Though the phrase "great concern for my health" sounds strangely formal, the repetition of the question "where is your head" grounds listeners in a much more relatable place.

lang's three-part harmony, all recorded by her on the track, further reiterates the different voices in her head. Mink's violin and Teddy Borowiecki's piano support lang throughout the track. A stripped-down video version of the song (with the prominent MTV logo in the upper right corner) shows lang singing while playing guitar, with Mink on violin, and Borowiecki on piano.[7] Performed as a trio without percussion, the quiet power of the song is revealed, and may even be preferable to the way it was recorded for the album.

Although "Mind of Love" was released as the second single for *Ingénue*, after the mega-hit "Constant Craving," it didn't gain much notoriety. Instead, it was breezed over for the hilariously campy "Miss Chatelaine," the next song—and hit—from the record.

Track 3. "Miss Chatelaine"

Shimmering twelve-string guitar, Mink's ever-present violin, and Teddy Borowiecki's introductory accordion set the scene for "Miss Chatelaine," a campy romp through lang's teenage memories of *The Lawrence Welk Show*. It both parodies and praises variety show and drag show performances. The track serves as much-needed comic relief, and one can easily imagine lounging on a couch, drinking a martini, and watching it performed on an old black-and-white TV set.

---

[7] "k.d. lang—The Mind of Love (live 92)." *YouTube*, uploaded by The lang Channel, n.d. https://www.youtube.com/watch?v=9o5dwZ8MJ-U.

After performing "Chatelaine" live on the BBC in 1993, she sat down with Alan Titchmarsh, "I am in love with accordion, and I love very much my accordion player, so I put my influences and my romantic sounds of what I am inspired by in my music."[8]

In an attempt to satirize herself at the hilarity of becoming Canadian magazine *Chatelaine*'s "Woman of the Year" in 1988, the song and the personae of lang in drag as "Miss Chatelaine" was born. On Twitter in 2016, k.d. posted the 1988 *Chatelaine* cover photo and recalled how they airbrushed the lipstick on. "FYI. The lipstick was airbrushed on. #gottaprotectmybutchness."[9] Many of the song lyrics ponder, though performed with feigned modesty, why lang would have ever been chosen as a *Chatelaine*'s Woman of the Year:

I can't explain/
Why I've become Miss Chatelaine . . .

Authors Hugh Barker and Yuval Taylor in their book *Faking It: The Quest for Authenticity in Popular Music* write about characteristics of camp, "Camp culture tends to celebrate manufactured poses and knowingly absurd pretenses as a deliberate response to the complexities of gay identity."[10] In

[8] "Miss Chatelaine / Constant Craving & Interview - 1993." *YouTube*, uploaded by The Lang Channel, n.d. https://www.youtube.com/watch?v=Qqo6xaiFky8.

[9] lang, k.d. [kdlang]. *Twitter*. November 24, 2016. https://twitter.com/kdlang/status/801848405794267136?lang=en.

[10] Barker, Hugh and Yuval Taylor. *Faking It: The Quest for Authenticity in Popular Music*. New York: Norton, 2007, 237.

one of her greatest live performances of "Chatelaine," on the *The Arsenio Hall Show* in 1993, lang epitomizes these "absurd pretenses."

When the *Arsenio* performance begins, so do the endless stream of bubbles that surround lang and the band. Mink's violin, coupled with the accordion, takes listeners to dizzying heights from the onset. Sitting downstage, and lounging on a red velvet chaise lounge, is none other than "Miss Chatelaine," a.k.a. lang in "drag." Drag, for lang as a butch lesbian, is high femme—she wears full makeup, an updo wig, and a lemon chiffon gown with a matching shawl.

In many ways, this "Chatelaine" performance and French influence recall the playful theatricality of Julie Andrews singing "Le Jazz Hot" in the gender-bending movie musical *Victor/Victoria* (1982). Andrews plays Victoria, a destitute singer who meets a gay man, nicknamed "Toddy" (Robert Preston), who devises a plan for Victoria to dress up as a man and then perform in "drag" at the fictional Club Chez Lui. In typical musical comedy fashion, madness and mayhem ensue.

When lang's performance of "Chatelaine" inevitably ends, the crowd claps and "woofs," as was part of the *Arsenio* show schtick. Hall then shouts, "Is *that k.d.*?!" and invites her over for an awkwardly hilarious, and later more poignant, interview. Since this was lang's second appearance on *Arsenio*, and the first was in 1990, during the *Torch and Twang*-Reclines era of her career, her new persona as "Miss Chatelaine" seemed to genuinely confuse the host.

Unsure whether lang has truly "become Miss Chatelaine," as the song lyrics state, Hall sizes her up. He begins first by pointing out her cleavage and compliments her, "You look very pretty." lang, ever an actor, plays it up as if she's flattered.

Hall asks "What's next?" for the then 32-year-old lang. lang quips "industrial punk . . . or I might do an exercise record." Before cutting to a commercial, Hall turns to the crowd and says, "I'm gonna invite her over during the commercial to watch *The Playboy Channel* with me." This seems to acknowledge that Hall is aware, somewhat, of her putting him on. The innuendo of inviting lang to watch "*Playboy*" with him also indicates his knowledge of her sexuality.

After the break, she returns on a more serious note. Hall asks lang her feelings about the new president-elect, Bill Clinton. lang politely reminds Arsenio she is Canadian, which the audience gives a big round of applause for, and then says she hopes the energy Clinton has will move things forward for the United States and elsewhere. Then Hall shifts to discuss Colorado, where in December of 1992 a vote passed denying gays protection from discrimination:

"What do you think of that?" he asks lang.

"It's 1993, and people are still quibbling about whether gays should have rights!"

Only a few people in the crowd clap, and Hall comments cleverly, "Not as much applause [for gay rights] as for Canada." He understands the gravity of their sudden silence. He then does some physical comedy to relieve the tension: he puts out his hands, but one much higher than the other, and pretends to clap. While this is a small thing, it does indicate how he's trying to keep the audience interested, but also wants to call them out.

In 1990, Arsenio was confronted head-on by Queer Nation protestors who attended a taping of the show. They interrupted Hall to question why he didn't have any openly gay guests on the show. Hall was defensive, "You think I haven't had someone on the show because they're gay? What's wrong with you?" He said many guests weren't out and didn't want to openly talk about their sexuality on the show. Elton John was the example that Hall provided of a gay star who'd performed there and "rocked the house." Later in the same episode, the protestors interrupted him again to ask why he was making jokes at the expense of gays. He'd stated that he does characters, not anti-gay jokes. Since then Hall has remarked that there is bigotry on both sides of the argument.[11]

Track 4. "Wash Me Clean"

The painfully slow and dreamy-sexy track "Wash Me Clean," which is the only with lyrics written by k.d. alone, has some of the clearest messages of lang's vulnerability. Mink plays bass on the track, as well as electric and acoustic guitars. Leisz's pedal steel is almost imperceptible, and Burton switches over to the marimba.

---

[11]Kinser, Jeremy. "Arsenio Hall Explains His Notorious On-Air Argument with Gay Rights Activists." *Queerty.* August 7, 2013. https://www.queerty.com/arsenio-hall-explains-his-notorious-on-air-argument-with-gay-rights-activists-20130807.

Lyrically, the person lang loves is "swim[ming] through" lang's "veins" like a drug, and she is "drowning" from her emotional addiction. Enveloped by lang's voice, listeners may envision swimming in slow motion while lang text paints plunging into the dark depths of her desire.

The second verse continues to reel us in:

> My desire carries no shame/
> My will, will harbor no pain/
> Wash, wash me clean/
> Mend my wounded seams/
> Cleanse my tarnished dreams

Even though her "desire carries no shame," she is still asking to be "cleansed." The activity of washing is typically done alone—unless one is a child or is in need of care. In a baptismal sense, cleansing will absolve from her "desire" even though she claims to not have shame. From the queer perspective, there is a great deal of pride in that statement. She does not need to feel shameful about her feelings of desire. The "seams" of lang have been wounded, which inverts the idea that stitches in seams are what hold pieces of cloth together. Instead, she is torn open. Her "dreams" or fantasies feel "tarnished." Something, usually an object, becomes tarnished after its exposure to too much moisture. Since water and wetness also depict erotic connotations, "wash me clean" then becomes an overarching sexual metaphor.

By the fourth track, listeners may want to protect lang from all this heartache. Why would she relinquish all control to someone who didn't love her back? But as most humans know, emotions—and sexual desire—despite our best efforts, tend to override logic.

Track 5. "So It Shall Be"

"So It Shall Be," cowritten by lang and Greg Penny, is one of the weaker tracks on the album. Though the song's introduction paces itself nicely, with isolated percussion first, then bass, and then lang's vocals, it lacks the lyrical depth of the other tracks. Not until the second verse, when Burton's vibes join in, and Piltch's bass becomes more pronounced, does the song become more intriguing. Additional percussion, along with accordion, electric guitar, and Mink's violin, are added in the third verse.[12]

Lyrically, lang and Penny set up a light and dark metaphor, an overused but accessible idea. The metaphor is dropped suddenly during the chorus creating a feeling of disjointedness between the parts of the song. The highlights of "So It Shall Be" include the jazzy three-part harmony in the third verse, Burton's vibes, but most notably Mink's ability to make his violin somehow sound like a medieval sitar.

[12]Awkwardly, the refrain in the chorus "Ask it and so it shall be" feels reminiscent of "So let it be written, so let it be done," a line from Cecil B. De Mille's 1956 film *The Ten Commandments* spoken by actor Yul Brinner, playing Pharaoh Ramses II.

Track 6. "Still Thrives This Love"

Ingénue's Latin influence is surfaces on the sixth track of the album. The sheet music notes this should be played in a "moderate bolero." As Felix Contreras of NPR explained, the "bolero" is a "form of love song that originated in Cuba in the 19th century. It came into its own after mostly Mexican composers, working in the 1940s, wrote songs that became popular throughout the Spanish-speaking world. The lyrics often reflect themes of bittersweet, unrequited, betrayed, or eternal love."[13]

The instrumentation and lyrics fall exactly into Contreras's definition. The use of the conga drum, rather than a drum kit, supplies a cool rhythmic groove, and the lyrics reinforce the theme of unrequited love:

> I often wonder, Is it so?/
> All I am holding wants to let go/
> How could I manage? I don't know/
> But still somehow thrives this love . . .

The introduction of the song has strong instrumental momentum for the first twenty seconds or so. Guitar, mandolin, bowed cello, and bass feel a bit overpowering when considering the verses and loungy vocal performance that follows. In a similar fashion to the previous track, "So It Shall Be," it feels like two separate ideas that haven't quite fused together. The middle section in between

---

[13]Contreras, Felix. "Canciones De Amor: Boleros for Your Lover." *NPR*, National Public Radio. February 14, 2008, https://www.npr.org/.

verses one and two features a guest clarinet player, Myron Schultz. During live performances, Mink replicated the clarinet sound with an effect on his violin. In the second verse, the piano is more pronounced. A cyclical return to the introduction comes in again after the chorus, and the accordion is now layered in with the clarinet as the song enters its third and final verse.

Structurally, this is a solid song with great instrumental and vocal performances. Though what comes next on the album, aside from the hits "Constant Craving" and "Chatelaine," may be the album's strongest.

Track 7. "Season of Hollow Soul"

Where the fifth and sixth tracks of the album lack, "Season of Hollow Soul" makes up for it. Often overlooked for the commercially pleasing "Craving" and "Chatelaine," "Hollow Soul" stands out as one of the most powerful, yet lesser-known, tracks on *Ingénue*. It's a moody, low-end driven piece with bass, piano, keys, violin, cello, clarinet, and, of course, lang's miraculous voice.

The start of the song was described by *Pulse!* as "like Angelo Badalamenti's *Twin Peaks* incidental music for Audrey Horne."[14] It does hold a mysterious, noir-ish quality that fits that description.

---

[14]Bireley, Nesbitt. *Pulse!*. April 1992.

The first verse and chorus have stripped-down instrumentation to showcase lang's voice. Mink leads into the second verse with an effect on his violin that enhances the melancholy mood of the song. As the band leads into the second chorus, there are dramatic drum flourishes, guitar and piano chords that drive the song forward, and harmonies supplied by multiple tracks of k.d.'s voice, particularly as she builds to the chorus:

Fate must have a reason/
Why else endure the season/
Of hollow soul

In 2018, on PBS's *Landmarks- Live in Concert* series, lang performed the *Ingénue* album for her twenty-fifth anniversary redux tour in chronological order. Before diving into "Hollow Soul," she delivered a dramatic monologue of sorts to introduce the song, which highlights both the song's beginnings and her current life as a Buddhist:

When I was writing "Ingénue" I was living in Vancouver. . . . Every day I would walk in this beautiful park off downtown, Stanley Park, searching for the muse . . . every day I would pass this huge fallen cedar tree . . . and straddling its carcass were two verdant, beautiful, young cedar trees—feeding off the nutrients of impermanence.[15]

---

[15]"Great Performances: k.d. lang—Landmarks Live in Concert." *PBS.* December 14, 2018. https://www.pbs.org/wnet/gperf/k-d-lang-landmarks-live-in-concert-a-great-performances-special-about/9068/.

While it's easy to note how the song is about surviving heartache, her tale of walking through the scenic Stanley Park in Vancouver adds rich context. Listeners can sense her isolation as she "endure[s] the season of hollow soul" as the lyrics put it.

The environmental imagery is also accentuated after hearing her story. Phrases like "uprooted chance" and "grains of goodbye" hint at her connection with the life cycle of the natural world, living and dying, and facing our own mortal "impermanence."

Ironically, lang breaks into a sing-songy "La, la, la, la, la-la, la," which feels painfully taunting in the middle of such a heavy tune. At that moment, she calls to mind "La La Lu" by Peggy Lee, one of her vocal influences, a track that was featured famously in Disney's 1955 film *Lady and the Tramp*.

More surprisingly, "Soul" is reminiscent of the ending of ABBA's "Chiquitita" from their 1979 album *Voulez-Vous*. While it might take several listens to hear how the two are similar, the final instrumental portion of the Swedish pop band's hit shares a similar chord progression, and percussive elements, to the chorus of "Hollow Soul."

Track 8. "Outside Myself"

"Outside Myself" features Mink on a twelve-string guitar, as well as Leisz on lap steel, Borowiecki on piano, keys, and accordion, and Piltch on a Yamaha BB 300 fretless bass. The steady pace kept by the piano as the song builds drives the song forward. Small flourishes throughout by Leisz and Piltch add to the already stunning instrumentation.

lang delivered possibly her best live rendition of both "Outside Myself" and "Hollow Soul" on BBC Two's *Later . . . with Jools Holland* in 1992.[16] On *Holland*, there is a slower tempo than the album, but it seems to fit the song's lyrics that depict a person moving through the world slowly, learning to attach to others, but struggling with feelings of separateness:

> I've been outside myself for so long/
> Any feeling I had is close to gone . . .

lang's lyrics are both meditative and reflective throughout. When listening, the elongation of the words "outside myself" emphasized by the three-part harmony references outsiderness that stands in for sexuality in this case. It may resonate most with LGBTQ+ listeners, particularly those who struggle to express their sexuality publicly.

Many queer-identified people find themselves living in reaction to others, from the outside in, rather than embodying themselves and living from the inside out. In this way, many queers are prepared to defend themselves from external or societal scrutiny. "Outside," in this case, could also be viewed as society judging lang (or her judging herself).

The vocal harmonies on the track and the piano work, nestles in sweetly to the 12/8 time signature. Another excellent rendition of the song can be seen on the recording of the twenty-fifth-anniversary *Ingénue Redux* concert. Piltch, who

---

[16]"k.d. lang, Outside Myself and Season of Hollow Soul." *YouTube*, uploaded by rocky storm. n.d. https://www.youtube.com/watch?v=_DTEN858KKM.

rejoined k.d. for the anniversary, has an outstanding electric bass solo that adds new dimension to the end of the track.

During the writing of the album, lang also performed in an independent film called *Salmonberries* (1991). The film's set is predominantly in Alaska and depicts the relationship between lang's character, Kotzebue, and a widow named Roswitha. Though the film is slow-paced, dimly shot, and difficult to follow, the pining of lang's character for Roswitha mimics lang's real-life heartache that inspired *Ingénue*. The subject matter coupled with the frigid cold of filming in Alaska helped to inspire the album, and perhaps even the icy/cold imagery of "Outside Myself."

Track 9. "Tears of Love's Recall"

The torch ballad "Tears of Love's Recall" is a another dip on the album, but it may be that way because it is wedged between two much stronger tracks, "Outside Myself" and lang's most recognizable hit "Constant Craving."

Lyrically abstract, "Tears" is challenging to connect with, as seen in the chorus:

The tears of love's recall/
Like blood to chocolate, fall

The odd syntax of the words, "like blood to chocolate, fall," does not seem to land. Additionally, the chorus is punctuated with a strange "drip" sound from a synthesizer that plainly doesn't fit. Had the dripping effect started earlier and been layered quietly throughout in a less obvious way, it's possible it might have worked. Instead, it calls to mind a boom mic accidentally dropping into the shot of an important period piece. It is one of the only indications of the album's decade in which it was made. As Mink stated previously, the instruments were painstakingly selected to create a "timelessness," ultimately, so one has to wonder why this "drip" made the final cut.

Worth checking out is how the track finally got its due during the *Ingénue Redux* concert, where pianist Daniel Clarke adds much-needed complexity to the song during the live performance.

Track 10. "Constant Craving"

The first time I heard "Constant Craving" on the radio I was sitting in the back of our family's red Pontiac Sunbird station wagon. I was fifteen. My father was driving. Thankfully, after purchasing the car without a radio, my dad had finally installed one. I recognized something familiar in the singer's voice. I asked my father, who was driving, to turn up the volume for the second verse as it led into the chorus:

Maybe a great magnet pulls/
All souls towards truth/
Or maybe it is life itself/
That feeds wisdom to its youth

A shock went through my entire body. I wanted to cry, and I didn't understand why.

As the late neurologist Oliver Sacks's describes in his essay "Lamentations: Music, Madness, and Melancholia," from his 2007 book *Musicophilia: Tales of Music and the Brain*, emotional responses that people experience when listening to music can be transformative, especially in times of distress. Sacks's uses an excerpt from William Styron's memoir *Darkness Visible* (1990) as an example. Styron was on the verge of suicide one night, was apathetic about a movie he'd put on to distract himself. Then, Styron heard the Brahms's Alto Rhapsody playing during one of the scenes. "This sound, which like all music—indeed, like all pleasure—I had been numbly unresponsive to for months, pierced my heart like a dagger."[17]

Since the DJ didn't announce who sang "Craving," and this was pre-internet, I resorted to waiting by my clock radio to hear the song again. And boy, did I hear it. And hear it. And hear it. Soon enough, all the pieces lined up. It was lang alright. After that, lang was the lighthouse, and "Craving" was a beacon of hope to escape the murky waters of adolescent queerness.

No one was prepared for the success of "Constant Craving," nor was it an instant hit. Not until its release in North America did the song find its audience. When contrasted with the rest of the album, "Craving" had the ability to be marketed as a single. Because of this, lang wanted to throw "Craving" away. As Mink revealed during our interview, "k.d. does better

[17]Styron as qtd. in Sacks. Sacks, Oliver. *Musicophilia*. New York: Vintage Books, 2007, 325.

things that she throws in the garbage than most people will ever do in their lives."

lang felt the song sounded too commercial in contrast with the rest of the album's melancholy mood. In interviews, she admitted that "Craving" made her feel a little like a sellout, but the album needed a tenth track:

> [k.d.] didn't really like the song, thinking it was "too commercial . . ." It didn't help that it was tracked originally in a different key. k.d. wanted to trash it quite early . . . but Marc [Raemer] and Greg [Penny] and I really believed in it, and I remember staying up really late one night and re-tracking all the guitars in a different key, and that put the song back in the running.[18]

The record company also sensed it was a hit single, but still lang resisted. Also, k.d was struggled to write lyrics for a third verse. Penny elaborated on how lang's frustration with the song derailed a recording session:

> [k.d.] was trying to finish off the third verse . . . I'm in the control room, and there's no sightline for me to see her, but she says . . . [on the talkback], "Give me a minute" . . . I call Ben [Mink] and say, "What do you think?" And he says, "Let her have time, let her do her thing" . . . I wait . . .

[18]Mink, Ben as qtd. in Jackson. Jackson, Blair. "Classic Track: 'Constant Craving,' k.d. lang." *Mix Magazine Online.* August 1, 2013.

then I stand up and look and she's gone! I walk out to the car park and her car is gone.[19]

Since lang's struggles with "Craving" persisted, Mink cleverly offered to add a guitar solo to fill the gap; "Craving" is one of the only tracks on *Ingénue* without a third verse.

Musically, "Craving" is gorgeous. The famous accordion riff, played by Borowiecki on a 1960s Hohner Morino VM and Mink strumming along on his acoustic coupled with lang's smooth vibrato, produces the track's signature sound. Vocally, for most of the track, lang stays in a lower register. Not until the bridge, on the lyrics "Ah, ha . . ."—as if she's pieced together a mystery—k.d. shows off a slightly higher range, with the former Reclines' background vocalist Sue Leonard hitting the high harmony. Throughout the chorus, Mink on violin adds elements of text painting, bowing in a steady "marching beat" to emphasize the lyrics ". . . someone always marches brave / here beneath my skin . . ." Overall, Mink's musical contributions to arrangements of preexisting demo tracks, particularly his work on "Craving," cannot be overstated.

Lyrically, reiterating the word "maybe" throughout "Craving" makes the whole song feel like a philosophical meditation. In a 2017 interview with *The Guardian*, k.d. connected it to her Buddhist practice:

[19]Penny, Greg as qtd. in Jackson. Jackson, Blair. "Classic Track: 'Constant Craving,' k.d. lang." *Mix Magazine Online.* August 1, 2013. https://www .mixonline.com/recording/classic-track-constant-craving-kd-lang-366433.

"Constant Craving" relates to samsara, the Buddhist cycle of birth and death, but I wasn't a practicing Buddhist then so I honestly don't know what the impetus for the song was. I just wrote it from the perspective of desire and longing.[20]

She also admitted that the original sound of "Craving" was partially inspired by listening to the chords and the arrangement of Joni Mitchell's "Black Crow" from *Hejira* (1976). Coincidentally, Mitchell's *Hejira*, like *Ingénue*, was also a musical departure. Mitchell had started to move away from her trademark folk-flower child sound to jazz on 1975s *The Hissing of Summer Lawns*, but not until *Heijra* did it seem fully realized.

Mink agreed that "Craving" was a game-changer, "When DJs in America started playing ["Craving"], the Warner Brothers switchboard lit up with people calling in. Having such a big hit was life-changing."[21]

Now imagine one of the biggest rock bands of all time accidentally steals your song. This happened with the Rolling Stones and "Constant Craving."

In 1997, just five short years after *Ingénue*'s release, "Craving" was subconsciously lifted by the Rolling Stones. Their single "Anybody Seen My Baby" accidentally borrowed the melody from the chorus of "Craving."

[20]lang, k.d. as qtd. in Simpson. "kd lang and Ben Mink: How We Made 'Constant Craving.'" *The Guardian*. September 26, 2017.

[21]Mink, Ben as qtd. in Simpson. "kd lang and Ben Mink: How We Made 'Constant Craving.'" *The Guardian*. September26, 2017.

Mink tells me that he seems to have foreshadowed this event long before it actually happened when joking with a friend:

> We used to joke, "One day the Stones are gonna listen to our music and they're gonna take something from ours." Then how many years go by? And I get a call from my lawyer one morning. She says, "Are you sitting down? . . . I just got a call from the Rolling Stones' manager. They have a record coming out Monday, and a new single. The video is all done. Everything's all done. Keith's daughter heard the single on the weekend. She said, "Daddy, that's 'Constant Craving.'"

Keith Richards also recounted this event in his 2010 memoir *Life*: "My daughter Angela and her friend were at Redlands and I was playing the record and they start singing this totally different song over it. They were hearing K.D. Lang's 'Constant Craving.' It was Angela and her friend that copped it."[22]

To avoid a lawsuit, the Stones—who rarely include others in their compositions—offered to add songwriting credits to both lang and Mink; they graciously accepted the offer.

[22]Richards, Keith. *Life.* New York: Little, Brown & Company, 2010.

7
Critics and Coming Out

Even though lang had expressed in interviews that country music was a "love affair that had ended,"[1] some critics still pummeled *Ingénue* with their reviews. Many said the genre switch was too great a departure for once-cowboy-punk "Torch and Twang" singer from Canada, but k.d. says country music *was* the departure, and pop was a homecoming.[2] Her repertoire was expanding and so was her audience.

When asked about this for the BBC, lang stated, "I look at myself primarily as a vocalist, as a singer of songs, not a singer of a certain genre . . . [country music] was a passion that I really focused on for seven years during k.d. lang and

[1]"k.d. lang Interview on Sexuality, Patsy Cline, and Roy Orbison—*Later with Bob Costas*." *YouTube*, uploaded by ClevelandLiveMusic. April 28, 1992. https://www.youtube.com/watch?v=1LW4p7GLof8.

[2]"k.d. lang Thinks She's a 1 Hit Wonder." *YouTube*, uploaded by Q on CBC. February 27, 2017. https://www.youtube.com/watch?v=SuKfPqwitKk.

the Reclines, but like a lover the time has come where I had to say goodbye."[3]

In Shana Goldin-Perschbacher *Queer Country* (2022), the author mentions John Sloop's analysis of lang's switch from country to pop as a "lack of genre commitment."

"Sloop notes that although she was now out . . . her shift from low-cultural-value county music to higher-culture-value torch singing and easy listening led to approval from journalists."

First, in no way is *Ingénue* "easy listening," as Sloop says. The record is structurally, harmonically, and lyrically complex. Writing off *Ingénue* as "easy listening" is a poor attempt at diminishing its musical value. It also ignores the depth and artistry of lang and Mink, and even brings to mind the term "yacht rock," to describe the type of brainless music yuppies might listen to while adventuring on their expensive boats.[4]

Second, *Ingénue* did not receive "approval from journalists" initially. A few reviewers, in particular, criticized the move from country to pop while insulting both lang and Mink in the process. Mink recalled,

> It was not received well when it first came out. "Constant Craving" was released in Britain, and it didn't do a thing really. We got a review in *People* that just said, something like, "k.d., maybe next time Ben comes knocking on your door, RUN." I mean, it was just crazy. The A&R guy said,

---

[3]"Miss Chatelaine / Constant Craving & Interview—1993." *YouTube*, uploaded by The lang Channel. n.d. https://www.youtube.com/watch?v=Qqo6xaiFky8.

[4]"Sailing" by Christopher Cross (1979) is a prime example of "yacht rock."

"You know what, this is all good stuff." Then they released "Constant Craving" in North America, and our world changed. It just started taking off.[5]

In an interview on Q on CBC, lang mentioned,

> I'm still very proud of [*Ingénue*] . . . Ben Mink, my writing partner and co-producer, [we] put our heart and soul into that record. We really didn't know what was gonna happen . . . if it was going to be well received . . . it wasn't at the beginning. It got slammed by some bad reviews. But it persisted.[6]

One of the critics who took aim at lang was Mike Joyce of *The Washington Post*. Joyce claimed lang owed a "debt" to her country fans and reduced *Ingénue* to "ballads of obsessive desire" with "emotionally despairing refrains." While obsessive desire is certainly there, it is also one of the key reasons listeners emotionally connect to the material. Also the album doesn't always despair—consider the playful romp of "Miss Chatelaine," for example.

Joyce also harped on lang's genre switch in a concert review, saying lang's live *Ingénue* performance was "all torch, no twang; all chanteuse, no cowgirl."[7]

---

[5]Mink, Ben. Personal Interview. Conducted by the author. December 3, 2021.

[6]"k.d. lang Thinks She's a 1 Hit Wonder." *YouTube*, uploaded by Q on CBC. February 27, 2017. https://www.youtube.com/watch?v=SuKfPqwitKk.

[7]Joyce, Mike. "K.D. lang." *The Washington Post*. July 13, 1992. https://www.washingtonpost.com/archive/lifestyle/1992/07/13/kd-lang/efd73f5b-07da-4c73-9603-2a0e560c2138/.

On the other hand, *The Los Angeles Times* at least acknowledged lang's difficulties in country music, "For seven years, k.d. lang was the odd woman out in country" and mostly embraced the "new musical direction" of *Ingénue*:

[*Ingénue* is] an often melancholy mood piece with Latin, continental, and jazz flavors . . . a flat-out d-i-v-o-r-c-e from Nashville, with Piaf replacing Patsy. . . . After years of "is she or isn't she" speculation, lang unburdened herself in an interview in the June 16 issue of the Advocate, speaking publicly for the first time about her homosexuality.[8]

In *Pulse!*, which was a publication of Tower Records, Nesbitt Bireley gushed over *Ingénue*:

Great albums are a collection of first-rate tunes that hang together thematically . . . a really great album will also have a coherent emotional flow . . . have emotional resonance, which reveal new facets each time you play them . . . [*Ingénue*] ranks among the greatest pop albums ever made.[9]

In recent years, when weighing *Ingénue* as a classic album, *Pitchfork*'s Laura Snapes gave the album a 9 out of 10. Snapes also used a more contemporary lens to acknowledge the daunting emotional state lang was in at the time:

---

[8]Cromelin, Richard. "POP MUSIC: For k.d. Lang it's Bye-Bye, Patsy— Hello, *Ingénue.*" *Los Angeles Times.* August 2, 1992. https://www.latimes.com/archives/la-xpm-1992-08-02-ca-5557-story.html.

[9]Bireley, Nesbitt. *Pulse!.* April 1992.

She was irrevocably in love with a married woman, and there was nothing she could do. . . . The crush was a lost cause, and despite heavy rumors about her sexuality and a much-remarked-upon lesbian contingent in her fanbase, lang was also not yet officially out.[10]

Certainly, lang's albums prior to *Ingénue* also displayed the singer's vulnerability. *Torch and Twang* was filled with it on tracks like "Trail of Broken Hearts," which looks back on a broken relationship, but *Ingénue*—based on the lyrics alone—was, indirectly, her way of coming out *before* publicly announcing it.

Coming Out in *The Advocate*

On June 16, 1992, just a few months after *Ingénue*'s release, k.d. lang publicly came out in the popular LGBTQ+ magazine *The Advocate*. Lang recalls, "I was probably going to be outed by Queer Nation. I thought it would be the most responsible thing to do, just say 'I'm gay.' I did risk *Ingénue*. It was on the line."[11]

My best friend Beth and I were two closeted fifteen-year-old queers walking through a mall in suburban Rochester, New York, when she told me the news.

---

[10]Snapes, Laura. "k.d. lang: Ingénue." *Pitchfork*. September 8, 2019. https://pitchfork.com/reviews/albums/kd-lang-Ingénue/.

[11]"60 Minutes Australia: Craving More (2017)." *YouTube*, uploaded by 60 Minutes Australia. March 3, 17. https://www.youtube.com/watch?v=03VU0rGeHXI.

"Did you hear k.d. lang is gay?"

"WHAT?" I replied with feigned shock.

We broke into uneasy, excited laughter.

My point was, lesbians—and maybe everyone else—already knew, undeniably, that k.d. lang was a lesbian. I was surprised, however, that k.d. had finally announced it publicly. lang faced disapproval from many people in the gay community for not admitting it earlier, though she says she was never hiding it.

Reflecting on this, Canada's *IN Magazine*, celebrated the thirtieth anniversary of lang's announcement: "lang was one of the first to openly celebrate their sexuality—at a time when doing so was almost unthinkable . . . the bold move predated Ellen DeGeneres' famous 'Yep, I'm gay!' *Time* magazine cover . . . and turned the Canadian icon into the world's most visible lesbian."[12]

"[The year I won for *Ingénue*] 1992 is the year I came out as gay," lang explained in an interview with *The Guardian*, "When we went to the Grammys, religious groups were picketing outside."[13] Even protests couldn't stop the love from pouring in.

When *Ingénue* was released in 1992, lang's music and "lesbian chic" image finally synced up with the mainstream.

---

[12]"Flashback: k.d. lang Comes Out on the Cover of The Advocate Magazine, June 16, 1992." *IN Magazine*, Elevate Media Group Inc. June 16, 2022. https://inmagazine.ca.

[13]lang, k.d. as qtd. in Simpson. "kd lang and Ben Mink: How We Made 'Constant Craving'." *The Guardian*. https://www.theguardian.com/music /2017/sep/26/kd-lang-ben-mink-how-we-made-constant-craving.

While this recognition of sexuality in the media felt a little like progress, it was not without a downside. The lesbian chic aesthetic from the early 1990s tended to embrace displays of femme-on-femme sexuality but effectively erased those who identified as butch. While it is true that lang began to turn down the volume of her butchness during the time of *Ingénue*—as she grew her hair out, styled it more consciously, wore makeup, and for a brief time M.A.C. cosmetics even sponsored her—her move toward a less butch-presenting gender expression still didn't mean that she wasn't internally butch.

In August of 1993, lang clarified her thoughts on lesbian chic in *Rolling Stone*, "I'm a singer; that's what I am foremost. With the lesbian chic stuff, I feel like I'm being used as a representation when I didn't come out for any other reason but to alleviate a lot of personal pressure. This is just something that I want to say."[14]

While lang's "masculine" side may have been less obvious to her newer fans, it was there nonetheless. Most fans who had followed k.d.'s career from the start also seemed to understand that she was incapable of being pigeonholed one way or another.

As lang stated previously, she wanted to be considered a singer before anything else, and the sheer musicality of her voice is the focal point of the album around which all the other parts revolve.

---

[14]lang, k.d. as qtd. in Udovitch. "k.d. lang." *Rolling Stone*. August 5, 1993, 55–7.

Billboard magazine wrote about lang's "victory" in earning the Grammy for Best Pop Vocal Artist. "Her victory has resulted in platinum sales of her album, *'Ingénue,'* which features the award-winning song ['Craving']. Critics believe that lang's victory marks her transition from country to pop genre. However, lang's peers and fellow musicians say that her victory shows that her talent transcends all genres."[15]

In contrast, just a few years earlier in 1990, shortly after lang's double Grammy win, but prior to *Ingénue* and coming out, lang endured a painful interview on CBS's *Face to Face with Connie Chung*. Without hesitation, Chung starts her interview by using language that today might be considered homophobic to address lang's physical appearance:

CHUNG. I'm kinda trying to figure out what this androgynous thing is with you . . .
LANG. Listen, I know what you're trying to say, but the thing is that assertiveness and self-confidence is viewed upon as male characteristics, which is bullsh – *[bleep]*
CHUNG. Right, so why do you have to dress like that?
LANG. I don't see why you shouldn't dress any way you want to.

Chung's attempt to discredit lang's identity does not work. Rather than recoiling at the interviewer's obvious disapproval, lang makes a strong point about perceived gender roles though her "bullshit" was bleeped out.

Later, Chung doubled down:

[15]Newman, Melinda. "Grammy Win Propels lang to Platinum Status." *Billboard*, vol. 105, no. 12, March 20, 1993, pp. 1+.

CHUNG . . . Do you think you're about as normal as you
used to be when people didn't shower attention on
you?

LANG. God, Connie, what is "normal," really? Life is so
completely bizarre that I don't know what normal is
. . . I think I'm still normal. I still go to the bathroom.
I still feel insecure, and I still fall in love. And I still
try to be nice, but sometimes I can't. I run out of
energy—so yeah, I'm still normal.

lang is visibly shaken but attempts to regain her composure
for the remainder of the excruciating interview. It's been
reported that Chung also faced discrimination throughout
her life as an Asian American journalist. Even so, the
implication that lang is somehow not normal is appalling.
When lang says Chung's first name, "Connie," it seems
to illustrate how lang is trying to appeal to Chung to quit
her cross-examination. Stating, "I still try to be nice, but
sometimes I can't" feels directed at Chung's ignorance and
her earlier insinuations about lang's androgyny. [16]

What this interview encapsulates in the frame of this book
is how far queer people have come since the early 1990s, but
also how much LGBTQ+ people have had to fight for their
right to exist. Even in today's culture, LGBTQ+ people are
still fighting.

[16]"kd lang Profile and Interview on Face to Face with Connie Chung 1990,
pt. 1 of 2." YouTube, uploaded by Abstorch. n.d. https://www.youtube.com/
watch?v=IJFMcTa1XnA.

In contrast to Chung, when late interviewer extraordinaire Barbara Walters asked whether lang was scared about how coming out would affect her career, lang asserted, "I had made the choice that my personal liberty and the emancipation that I've felt about coming out was more important to me."[17]

* * *

On my nineteenth birthday in 1995, I officially came out to my parents. My folks were visiting to see me perform in my college production of Caryl Churchill's *Mad Forest*. I played the part of a nurse who was shell-shocked during the 1980s Romanian revolution; I was about to experience my own version.

Before the show, I decided to take my parents on a tour of my barely livable off-campus apartment. Most of the time I spent in that house I focused on learning lines for plays, playing acoustic guitar, or smoking Parliaments on the roof outside my bedroom. Sometimes all three at once. They followed me up the winding, creaky hardwood steps and entered my bedroom.

I didn't have many decorations on the wall besides an advertisement I'd tore from an *Out* magazine. The ad was for the first gay mail-order clothing company called Don't Panic. The image was of the Mona Lisa wearing a t-shirt that read,

[17]"k.d. lang Interview—Barbara Walters 1993." *YouTube*, uploaded by The lang Channel. April 14, 2013. https://www.youtube.com/watch?v=wivERtlHPYA.

"Nobody knows I'm a lesbian." I liked it because it gave new meaning to the smirk on her face.

> My mother's eyes landed directly on Mona Lisa's t-shirt.
> "I don't get it. 'Nobody knows the Mona Lisa is a *lesbian*?'"
> Sweat started forming on my forehead.
> "It's just a picture, Mom."

I knew then that I had to tell her. I couldn't bury it again. I was terrified. My mom was a wild card, specifically when it came to judging "unconventional" lifestyles. She listened to the foul Dr. Laura on the radio at home, who once called gays "products of a biological disorder," so there was no telling how my mom might respond.[18]

> I knew that I was a lesbian, but I went for the middle ground.
> "I'm bisexual."
> "Bisexual? What does that word mean? What does that word mean?"
> Suddenly everything she said, she said twice. It was some sort of nervous echolalia.

At this point, my father gave me a reassuring pat on the back. I felt a tiny bit of relief. He could be compassionate and reassuring when I least expected it. My mother kept up her rapid-fire questions and criticisms.

---

[18]Schlessinger as qtd. in Ladd. "StopDrLaura.com." *Salon*. March 1, 2000. https://www.salon.com/2000/03/01/drlaura_2/.

"I want to know. I want to know, Joanna."

"It means that I've dated men and women, and I like both, okay?"

"I don't get it. I don't get it."

I managed to perform in the play that night, although I also cried miserably while trying to apply my stage makeup. Looking at myself in the dressing room mirror, I thought about how theater had become a way to avoid myself while still getting the attention I desperately needed. Even if my mother couldn't understand what I'd told her, at least I was beginning to understand it all myself.

8
MTV Mania

MTV Music Video Awards

The 1980s and 1990s were prime time for musicians to create offbeat MTV music videos to supplement their hit songs. Director Mark Romanek, who would also later go on to direct both films and other famous videos such as "Closer" by Nine Inch Nails and Michael and Janet Jackson's "Scream," took on k.d. lang's "Constant Craving."

Romanek's inspiration for the "Craving" video was Samuel Beckett's famous play *Waiting for Godot*. Beckett's play centers around two men who wait around for a man named Godot to show up for the entirety of the play while pontificating about larger themes of life and death. The result was a highly stylized black-and-white music video, starring k.d., looking remarkably like a young Elvis, lip-syncing while staring off into the distance. The shots of lang, who is seen first in the backseat of a car, then staring into a fishbowl, and later on a stage, are interspersed with shots of two men on stage performing a slapstick version of *Godot* for an audience to mixed reviews.

The majority of the video focuses on lang, sitting in a striped button-down shirt with a tiny bit of cleavage showing, in a backstage area filled with props while the play goes on. Periodically, a random shirtless boy in swimming goggles appears. The video visually resembles an old silent film, though the bizarre pantomiming of the actors is at times painful to watch. Nevertheless, the concept behind the video connects—at least in part—to the song's lyrics about unfulfilled desire. Even though "Craving" wasn't shown frequently on MTV, the video still won an MTV Video Music Award for Best Female Video.

Fellow Canadian Keanu Reeves presents the award and as k.d. makes her way to the stage, dozens of fans reach out their hands to touch her. For a minute, it's like watching footage of Beatlemania. Behind the podium on stage k.d. quips, "Even the Psychic Friends Network couldn't have predicted this," and then sarcastically thanks *House of Style*, an MTV show that focused on supermodels and then— seeming to remember that she should thank the director— acknowledges Romanek and Warner Brothers.[1] Watching k.d. in such contrived circumstances is both endearing and painful. After her career's humble indie beginnings, whether she liked it or not, she was now fully in the spotlight, and the attention kept rolling in.

[1]"k.d. lang—MTV Music Awards 1993." *YouTube*, uploaded by The lang Channel. June 1, 2013. https://www.youtube.com/watch?v=RUDXyavRYcw.

MTV *Unplugged*

MTV *Unplugged* was a commercial sensation that allowed MTV's core audience to see live performances without having to leave the couch. k.d. lang even took to the *Unplugged* stage in December 1992, in between two of *Unplugged* best-known performances, Eric Clapton in August 1992[2] and Nirvana in November 1993.[3] Later, k.d. joined Tony Bennett during his 1994 *Unplugged* concert to sing the duet "Moonglow." Her collaboration with Bennett ultimately led them to their 2002 Grammy Award-winning album, *A Wonderful World*.

In *Faking It: The Quest for Authenticity in Popular Music*, authors Barker and Taylor assert:

> "Unplugged" was conceived as a response to the public perception that the contemporary music scene was obsessed with image rather than content . . . artists would perform their songs preferably with only acoustic instruments or at least in a quieter, more stripped-down form; the audience could then judge whether or not these were musicians and singers who could really perform.[4]

[2] Clapton famously reworked Cream's "Layla" and the heartbreaking elegy to his son, "Tears in Heaven."

[3] *Unplugged* was one of Nirvana's last live shows, recorded just five months before Kurt Cobain took his own life; critics have praised it as one of the best live performances ever.

[4] Barker, Hugh and Yuval Taylor. *Faking It: The Quest for Authenticity in Popular Music*. Norton, New York, 2007.

The intimacy of k.d.'s *Unplugged* performance passed Barker and Taylor's aforementioned litmus test. Not only were lang's vocals nearly flawless, but the *Unplugged* concert also proved she could duplicate, and even surpass, the sound of the *Ingénue* album in a live setting. Fans who had followed lang's career from the start already knew her capacity for brilliant live shows, but her new school MTV recruits finally had the opportunity to hear it for themselves.

Even though *Ingénue* was a hit, her *Unplugged* recording wasn't available until 2017, when Nonesuch Records included it on a double LP for *Ingénue*'s twenty-fifth anniversary. It's surprising that it took decades to release, especially when reviewing the financial windfall of other recordings. For instance, Clapton's *Unplugged* sold 26 million worldwide and Nirvana's *Unplugged* went multiplatinum. Perhaps choosing to release it at a later time was an intentional choice, as tragedy factored into both Clapton and Cobain's performances, or maybe the choice was out of her hands.

Madonna and k.d.

Elvis is alive—and she's beautiful!
—*Madonna on k.d. lang*

Frequently paired together on MTV throughout the early 1990s, Madonna and lang were the hottest couple that never was. The pop superstar admitted that she felt k.d. resembled a young Sean Penn, who Madonna had been married to from

1985 to 1989, so rumors of an alleged lesbian relationship with lang abounded even before *Ingénue*.

At Madonna's *Truth or Dare* (1991) film premiere in Los Angeles, though Madonna and lang arrived separately, MTV cameras made sure to get a shot of k.d. walking down the red carpet. Afterward, with actress Julia Roberts mysteriously at lang's side, MTV asked for lang's thoughts on Madonna's film, to which she responded: "I think she is totally abusing the system and that's beautiful."[5]

As if a film and the upcoming 1992 *Erotica* album weren't enough, Madonna also turned her sexuality into a controversial coffee table book, *Sex*. One has to wonder how many cups of coffee were spilled while skimming the pages. The *Sex* book was filled with photographs of Madonna engaged in multiple sex acts, ranging from S&M to lesbian sex. *Sex* was located on the highest shelf above the adult magazines at bookstores. The brand new copies were wrapped in mylar paper, and they glistened from the vantage point staring upward. If you had the money to buy it, you would have to ask a cashier to get it down. Hormonal adolescents with no money like me had barely any chance to shoplift it.

With all of this brewing, Madonna took it a step further by expressing her attraction for k.d. in a 1991 interview with *The Advocate*: "k.d. lang [is] gorgeous, by the way . . . I met her, and I thought, Oh my God, she's the female version

[5]"Madonna's Truth or Dare Premiere Party - MTV Special - 1991 - Part 01." *YouTube*. uploaded by RetroSpectoVideos. February 25, 2013. https://www .youtube.com/watch?v=ma_T_javZFs.

of Sean. I could fall in love with her."[6] Since both lang and Madonna seemed unattached to anyone else at the time, and pop culture was suddenly hungry for lesbian content, the speculation continued.

Not long ago, k.d. lang claimed that the Madonna rumors shocked her back then, though it's somewhat hard to believe. It makes sense to imagine that lang would have had at least a vague awareness of how MTV and tabloids would run with it.

> I was surprised when I heard a rumor that I'd slept with Madonna . . . I was completely oblivious to it. . . . It's a byproduct of show business . . . that's one of the reasons I don't like participating in show business.[7]

Further, k.d. admitted that the rumored relationship was a "showmance" suggested by Madonna and lang's mutual publicist. After all, *Ingénue* was released a few months prior to Madonna's *Erotica*. "We shared a publicist . . . did the publicist decide to put [out] those rumors so they could both sell records? I don't know the entire story. Maybe."[8] Showmance or not, the two played off each other's success well, and fans of both Madonna and lang didn't seem to mind the fantasy.

[6]Shewey, Don. "Madonna: The X-Rated Interview." *The Advocate.* May 7, 1991.

[7]Hanra, Hanna. "'I Feel Exhausted by Being Exposed': kd lang on Being a Lesbian Icon." *The Guardian.* July 11, 2019.

[8]Toureille, Claire. "k.d. lang Hints Madonna Relationship Was a Showmance to Help 'Sell Records.'" *Daily Mail Online.* Associated Newspapers, June 16, 2019. https://www.dailymail.co.uk/ushome/index.html.

Melissa Etheridge, "the Other Gay Singer"

In a 1994 interview with *The Washington Post*, fellow out lesbian musician Melissa Etheridge hilariously referred to herself as "the *other* gay singer," implying k.d. was the original, if people happened to confuse the two.[9]

That same year, broadcast on MTV, Etheridge headlined at "The Beat Goes On" benefit concert for LIFEbeat for the organization's fight against AIDS. During the performance, k.d., who was waiting in the wings, was invited to share the stage with Etheridge for a duet of "You Can Sleep While I Drive." As a platonic pair, the two musicians played up their affection for the live audience who responded with hoots and hollers, and for those watching on the MTV broadcast at home.

"Let's hold hands for a minute. This is going to help our harmony . . ." lang said, grabbing hold of Etheridge's hand. Etheridge guffaws at this, then asks lang why the tabloids aren't spreading rumors about *them*, when they are spreading rumors about everyone else they think is gay. Quickly, lang replies, "Let's start some!"[10]

Shortly before the LIFEbeat concert, Bill Clinton was inaugurated. Without fail, MTV seized the opportunity to host the "Rock 'n' Roll Inaugural Ball." Later that night,

---

[9]Joyce, Mike. "Etheridge: Out and About." *The Washington Post*. July 6, 1994. https://www.washingtonpost.com/archive/lifestyle/1994/07/06/etheridge-out-and-about/9e02cbb4-b7da-4599-82fd-a3fe398a6787/.

[10]"Melissa Ethridge & KD Lang - You Can Sleep - The Beat Goes On - 1994." *YouTube*. Uploaded by LIFEbeat. n.d. https://www.youtube.com/watch?v=vE4nij3AZso.

the Triangle Ball was held, dubbed "the first such gala for homosexuals," by *The New York Times*.[11] Etheridge, following in k.d.'s footsteps, came out in public during the celebration.

A thirty-year-old video on YouTube shows Etheridge leading up to her announcement. k.d. stands directly behind Etheridge as she speaks, "I have to say, my sister k.d. lang has been such an inspiration. She's the greatest thing I've ever seen this year. I want to say now, I'm very proud that I've been a lesbian all my life." The crowd at the ball goes nuts, and lang is seen jumping up and down, and putting her fists in the air to celebrate.[12]

Vanity Fair Cover with Cindy Crawford

If Madonna's *Sex* book was literally and financially out of reach, *Vanity Fair* was ready to fill the void. Costing a mere *three* dollars in August 1993, at eye level on the magazine racks, lang was featured on the cover of *Vanity Fair* with supermodel Cindy Crawford. Every (closeted or not) queer teenager I knew back then, myself included, bolted to the bookstore to buy a copy (or two).

[11]Brown, Patricia Leigh. "THE INAUGURATION: Pomp, Patriotism, and Primping." *The New York Times*. January 21, 1993. https://www.nytimes.com/1993/01/21/us/inauguration-pomp-patriotism-primping-far-more-than-10000-maniacs-revel-capital.html.

[12]"Melissa Etheridge Coming Out" *YouTube*. Uploaded by sarah blyth. n.d. https://www.youtube.com/watch?v=74xbqclujJ4.

In the iconic shot, lang playfully smirks while leaning back in an old-fashioned barber chair to rest her head on Crawford's ample bosom. The supermodel holds a straight razor to lang's lathered-up throat as if she's about to shave lang. The cover was quickly torn off and taped to my bedroom wall when I got home. My mother was *not* pleased.

The photo was famously taken by Herb Ritts, although lang takes credit for the idea:

> We released "[Constant] Craving" as a single—then I did a photoshoot for Vanity Fair. I'd seen a French movie . . . and had this idea of being pictured in a barber's shop, so my friend Herb Ritts took a photograph of me being shaved by Cindy Crawford. . . . It caused a huge sensation . . . I'm very proud of that cover. I'm not sure "Craving" would have been such a big hit without it.[13]

The racy cover has had a long-standing cultural impact in the queer community for its subversiveness. lang and Crawford were notable celebrities who expressed gender and sexuality in juxtaposing ways. Crawford was immediately recognizable. She had been on magazine covers prior and famously featured with other supermodels walking down the runway in George Michael's "Freedom! '90" music video.

Alternately lang was less recognizable (at first). Covered in shaving cream, lang's face was turned inward, resting contentedly on Crawford's chest. Not until a person scanned

[13]Simpson, Dave. "k.d. lang and Ben Mink: How We Made Constant Craving." *The Guardian*. September 26, 2017. https://www.theguardian.com /music/2017/sep/26/k.d.-lang-ben-mink-how-we-made-constant-craving.

the text to the right of the image would they see the bolded words "k.d. lang's edge." That is when it crystallized for some: this seductive image was of a butch lesbian and a straight woman.

Since face shaving is traditionally reserved for men, viewers perceived lang in the stereotypically masculine role and Crawford in the feminine. The act of shaving in itself could be considered a pre-sex ritual, so the shaving—with a "straight" razor no less—has a dual meaning with the text "k.d. lang's edge," the razor in the image may be straight, but nothing else about the image is.

As Elliot asserts:

> This image created one of the most famous magazine covers of the 1990s and is worth a moment's reflection. It was a defining moment in the popularization of lesbian sexuality, a movement that began in the mid-1980s and is popularly known as "lesbian chic."

Though "lesbian chic" is a term fraught with contention, as previously discussed in Chapter 7, as Elliott describes, "Many lesbian political activists are uncomfortable with this [lesbian chic] phenomenon, which draws on conventional portrayals of femininity to privilege the image of feminine lesbianism at the expense of masculine lesbianism."[14]

In a 2015 interview, Crawford was asked if she thought the cover would be a "big deal" now:

[14]Elliott, Robin. "Performing k.d. lang." *Canadian Woman Studies*, vol. 24, no. 2–3, 5, winter–spring 2005.

I actually don't think it would be a big deal at all. . . . We're just exposed to so much these days . . . but, at the time, k.d. was just really coming out in a formal way, and they [Herb Ritts and lang] unbeknownst to me had this whole idea to play with gender stereotypes . . . I just trusted Herb so much . . . I was game.[15]

Ritts's *Vanity Fair* photo has also been recreated many times since 1993. Most recently, *RuPaul's Drag Race* star Shea Coulée took the place of Crawford, and creative director Scott Studeberg was in lang's position on the cover of *Out* magazine in 2020. Although the recreations take on a life of their own even out of context, the power of the original image will never fade.

[15]"A Conversation with Cindy Crawford: Clip 4 (On Iconic K.D. Lang Vanity Fair Cover Shoot)." *YouTube*, uploaded by Commonwealth Club of California. December 18, 2015. https://www.youtube.com/watch?v=b6BJmdClJ4k.

Part III
Post-*Ingénue*

9
Collaborators on k.d.

Keyboardist, multi-instrumentalist, and songwriter Daniel Clarke, who began performing with k.d. on the 2008 *Watershed* album and tour, was able to speak with me about his experiences working closely with lang. Clarke says initially that he got involved because lang's management asked him to record three songs on piano as a sort of audition:

> I did a laptop recording, and I guess k.d. dug them. Then I started doing a little research, and found out her piano player prior to me [Borowiecki] was an accordion player first . . . I thought of the riff in "Constant Craving," which is probably one of the best accordion riffs, but I'd never played accordion in my life! Then, one night, k.d. called on the phone. . . . After a little while, she asked, "Do you play accordion?" My answer should have been "No," but I said, "Like you've never heard!"

Clarke laughed infectiously remembering his answer and said he doesn't even think k.d. knows that story. He also recalls purchasing a $100 accordion on eBay after their conversation and "learning polkas like crazy." Ultimately, his hard work paid off, and Clarke ended up playing the "Constant Craving" riff.

Clarke also discussed how he felt one of k.d.'s greatest attributes was her ability as a bandleader. In particular, he pointed out her work on the *Watershed* album, "that music is so harmonically complex. And certainly melodically complex, but it's not jazz. That's a fine line—that's a hard, hard thing to do. I know that she always kind of, maybe, struggles with it in her head. She's always having a conversation with herself about this stuff."

He also confesses that since he's written with k.d. that he feels lang has opened him up as a musician. Their ability to improvise together, in particular, is how Clarke, who is steeped in music theory, was able to let go some of his musical rigidity:

> I might sit down to improvise, and afterward, she'd say, "What was that? What was right in the middle of that?" k.d. will say, "Okay, flip those two chords." In my brain, I'm sitting there, and smoke starts coming out of my ears. I'm thinking, "Oh, that's not gonna work." but k.d. got that out of me—and now I'm more open. A lot of people in her shoes just would have been like, "Alright, next!" But she was game to make this thing work.

In addition, Clarke mentions that k.d., too, is also great at improvising on the piano, "Sometimes, she would sit down and improvise for a minute, and she just has an incredible sense of form and development. She knows how to lay her hands when she sits down at a piano, and she just starts to kind of play shapes. It's crazy how good it is."

Lastly, Clarke discusses how he and lang have performed together as a duo for various events, but even though it is a whole other set of responsibilities, he still enjoys working with k.d., no matter where or what genre of music. "It speaks to what I love because I love all kinds of music. It's so nice to be able to do all of that with k.d."[1]

Drummer Fred Eltringham, who has been playing with Sheryl Crow since 2012 and formerly with the Wallflowers, and the [Dixie] Chicks, performed with k.d. on her thirteenth studio album, *Sing It Loud* (2011).

Eltringham joined lang's new band, the Siss Boom Bang, and recorded the album in Nashville. The sound was reminiscent of some of lang's earlier country work with the Reclines, though with a more alt-rock edge.

When speaking to Eltringham, he reminisced about how he was brought into play drums by Clarke and her pedal steel player, Joshua Grange (who had also played with the Chicks). Eltringham said the timing worked well for him, and he was excited for the opportunity to play alongside lang.

"While we were getting the Siss Boom Bang together, k.d. asked if I was still in the Wallflowers, but we were on hiatus and the band was deteriorating. So when k.d. asked, 'Do you want to tour for the record?' I just left the Wallflowers, and said, 'I'm gonna stay with k.d.'"

Eltringham says he loves playing with k.d. because she is an incredible person. "She's really sweet, and an amazing

[1]Clarke, Daniel. Personal Interview. Conducted by Joanna M. Stein. July 7, 2022.

singer, obviously . . . *Sing It Loud* was one of the best studio experiences I've ever had."

When inquiring why the studio experience was so great, Eltringham explained, "Just getting to record with k.d., and see how she does her thing," was inspiring for him. As an example, Eltringham discussed that after his experience with the Wallflowers, k.d.'s simplicity and ease with the recording process were refreshing, "When k.d. felt like she'd gotten her vocal performance down, then that was the take we used on the album."

Eltringham also described how lang, as a practicing Buddhist, prepared herself for going onstage when the Siss Boom Bang were on tour. "She's a Buddhist, so before each show, k.d. would just kind of center herself. She has these prayer beads to meditate, and get herself together. Then she comes out and kicks ass every single time. On stage, or in the studio, she always delivered."[2]

Prolific singer-songwriter/guitarist Laura Veirs also shared her experiences about recording and touring with k.d. and Neko Case for the group's eponymous album *case/lang/ veirs* (2016).

According to Veirs, the opportunity came together by chance. lang had met Neko Case around the same time that she was in Portland recording on Veirs' record *Warp & Weft* (2013). Soon after, k.d. emailed both of them with the idea for *case/lang/veirs*. Veirs, who had been a fan of *Ingénue* growing up, was thrilled to be invited to work with lang, "k.d. was one

---

[2]Eltringham, Fred. Personal Interview. Conducted by Joanna M. Stein. June 30, 2022.

of those artists that I remember really loving when I was 18. She was really groundbreaking with the gender bending and being the first queer woman out—the first queer pop star."

Veirs admitted feeling like most of the audience that came to see the trio perform were fans of k.d. or Neko, although Veirs had written every song on the *case/lang/veirs* album. Veirs mentioned that she needed to move past her insecurities, but she also contended with stage fright during their tour:

> We played in such big places that I had to get over it. It was very challenging for me psychologically to be up there. I was like "I don't know if I can do this. I literally don't know". . . . But k.d. and Neko were such confident performers; they didn't have stage fright at all. And they were so helpful [because] they just wanted to do the show and have fun. It kind of took the edge off.[3]

From interviewing her collaborators, it's obvious that those who have worked with lang more recently in music find her to be confident, centered, and helpful. This unique combination of attributes shows how there is both a joy and an ease to working with lang. It is no wonder, then, that lang's influence would extend far beyond music into other forms of entertainment as well.

[3]Veirs, Laura. Personal Interview. Conducted by Joanna M. Stein. June 6, 2022.

10
Pop Culture References

Both k.d. lang and *Ingénue*'s long-standing significance in pop culture is clear when viewing several contemporary TV series. Here is just a small sampling of the many references to both k.d. lang and "Constant Craving" in more recent years.

GLEE (2011)

In 2011, the TV show *GLEE* covered "Constant Craving." The episode, appropriately titled "I Kissed a Girl," was in the third season of the popular show that centers around a high school glee club and features many openly gay characters. Actress Naya Rivera, who played lesbian cheerleader Santana Lopez, sings the first verse. Once all the supportive head bobbing of fellow glee club members stops, the rendition is surprisingly moving, especially since Rivera's tragic death in 2020.

As with many of the renditions of classic songs on the show, several vocalists take turns singing the verses.

Rivera's character sings the introductory verse in the choir room while staring at her female love interest in the show. The second verse is in the capable hands of Broadway and Disney star Idina Menzel, who played Shelby Corcoran (a rival glee club coach).[1] As she sings, Menzel's character is seen cradling a three-ring binder while walking down the hallway of the fictional high school. She sings as an internal monologue, while controversially pining for the mohawked teen character, Puck (played by Mark Salling). Actor Chris Colfer's character is the openly gay Kurt Hummel, who picks up at the chorus toward the end of the song.

Later, lang would lend her voice to the series again in 2010 with a rendition of "You're a Mean One, Mr. Grinch" featured on Season 2, Episode 10, "A Very Glee Christmas." Though k.d. was not seen in the episode, her performance of the song fits the antics of Sue Sylvester (played by the one and only Jane Lynch) during the episode.

In the same year, at the Vancouver Olympics Opening Ceremonies, lang's jaw-dropping rendition of Leonard Cohen's "Hallelujah" would level everyone watching. Even though she had previously performed "Hallelujah" in front of the legendary singer-songwriter at Cohen's 2006 induction into the Canadian Songwriter's Hall of Fame, the international scope of lang's Opening Ceremonies performance brought her well-deserved newly found attention.

---

[1]Menzel originated the role of Maureen, a bisexual performance artist, in the 1996 Broadway smash, *Rent*.

Portlandia (2014)

In 2014, lang tried her hand at comedy in Season 4, Episode 10, "Getting Away," of the irreverent sketch comedy show *Portlandia* starring Fred Armisen, of *Saturday Night Live* fame, and Carrie Brownstein, actress (and also guitarist/singer from the Riot Grrrl band, Sleater-Kinney).

In the episode, lang plays a version of herself on a camping trip with a feminist group of women led by Armisen and Brownstein's characters, Toni and Candace, owners of the fictional feminist bookstore, Women & Women First. k.d. lang is first seen aboard the bus they've commissioned to go on their trip. The comedic premise then centers on actor/comedian Jason Sudeikis's character, Kim, who was mistakenly booked as a female bus driver. Toni and Candace ask "Where's Kim?" to which Sudeikis replies, "I'm Kim . . . short for Kimtofer."

A few scenes later, lang is seen strumming an acoustic guitar, while Toni and Candance become increasingly hostile toward Kim. Viewers can see lang holding back real laughter during one of the first scenes. Later, while the group sits around a campfire, Sudeikis's character admits, "I haven't had the best relationships with women romantically" to which lang responds, "If you ever want to know anything about women . . . you just call me. I know a lot about women." The bonding between the two characters eventually builds into the hilariously implausible: lang and Sudeikis becoming romantically involved, much to the chagrin of Toni and Candace. At the end of the episode, lang is seen leading the group out of the woods while playing guitar and singing "Down to the River to Pray."

"Constant Craving" on *Hacks* (2022)

In May of 2022, "Constant Craving" played a role in the hilarious comedy show, *Hacks*. Deborah Vance, played by Jean Smart, is a veteran celebrity comedian, and Ava Daniels, played by Hannah Einbender (an openly bisexual actress playing a bisexual character), plays Vance's new joke writer.

In Season 2, Episode 4, "The Captain's Wife," Deborah is accidentally booked to perform on a lesbian cruise, instead of a cruise with gay men. She says lesbians have never enjoyed her material and starts off both annoyed and fearful about how she'll be received by a lesbian audience. Ava, on the other hand, starts to live it up on the cruise. At one point, she has taken ecstasy, and the drug starts kicking in when she is having a discussion about sexuality with the typically close-minded Deborah. During their talk, "Constant Craving" starts playing on the ship:

AVA: You know what, Deborah? Your orientation isn't gay or straight. It's egomaniac.
DEBORAH: Ah, this waistband is kind of loose.
AVA: . . . Oh, no. [SIGHS] The Molly's hitting.
DEBORAH: What?
AVA: I might have to dance. —
DEBORAH: You did Molly?

[K.D. LANG'S "CONSTANT CRAVING" PLAYS]
AVA: (Singing) "Constant . . ."
DEBORAH: Okay, I can't watch this.
AVA: "Craving . . . Has always . . ." [GASPS] Oh, oh, is
   that a dolphin?[2]

Ava becomes so swept up in the song that she can no longer carry on a conversation. The song itself is so iconic and specific to lesbian culture that even playing it in the background becomes the focus of the scene.

Even though lang has stayed out of the spotlight for the past several years, there is no denying her cultural relevance every time she pops up, whether it be in song or in a TV cameo. In 2013, the power of her impact was celebrated when she was inducted into the Canadian Music Hall of Fame.

[2]"The Captain's Wife." *Hacks*. Created by Lucia Aniello, Paul W. Downs, and Jen Statsky, Season 2, Episode 4, Paulilu Productions, 2022.

11
Canadian Music Hall of Fame and *Ingénue*'s Twenty-Fifth Anniversary

In 2013, Canadian singer Anne Murray, best known for her 1978 hit "You Needed Me," introduced lang at the Canadian Music Hall of Fame award ceremony. In Murray's introductory speech, she reminisces about seeing lang for the first time in 1985; lang famously pranced up to the stage wearing a wedding dress and veil while accepting her first Juno award for "Most Promising Female Vocalist."[1]

"I loved her sense of fun, her spunk, her gumption, and she could sing," recalled Murray. "[k.d.] went on to show that a great voice could sing anything it wants. She defies labeling."[2]

Reminiscing about her first Juno on a 2021 segment for CBC, lang watches the video of herself accepting the award in

---

[1] The Juno is the Canadian equivalent of an American Grammy.

[2] "Singer k.d. lang on 'Letting Your Freak Flag Fly.'" *CBC News*. April 22, 2013.

a wedding dress and laughs, "I was injecting a lot of humor in it, but I was deeply, deeply moved. It was a very big moment for me."[3]

During lang's 2013 induction speech, she said,

Only in Canada could there be such a freak as k.d. lang receiving this award. . . . So I am here to tell you my friends and my countrymen that it is ok to be you, it is okay to let your freak flags fly and embrace the quirkmeister that's inside of all of us. And I'm not even just talking artists, I'm talking every single person in this nation has the right to be themselves, live life . . . I love you Canada, thank you so much.[4]

Ingénue's Twenty-Fifth Anniversary

For the twenty-fifth anniversary of *Ingénue* in 2017, a deluxe version of the album was re-released by Nonesuch Records. Finally included with the album, after all these years, was lang's *MTV Unplugged* performance. In 2017, lang also embarked on a multicity tour called the *Ingénue Redux* tour. A video of lang performing *Ingénue*, in chronological order, in its entirety, at the Majestic theater in San Antonio, Texas,

[3]"K.D. Lang Looks Back at Her Iconic Junos Win for Most Promising Female | Junos 50th." *YouTube*, uploaded by *CBC Music*. https://www.youtube.com /watch?v=wynWxugM8Bs&t=45s.

[4]"Singer k.d. lang on 'Letting Your Freak Flag Fly.'" *CBC News*. April 22, 2013.

was also made available. When viewing her performance at the Majestic, lang's calm is in such stark contrast from the wild physicality of her early career performances. When the lights come up, k.d. stands center stage in a full suit— barefoot. A practicing Buddhist now for roughly fifteen years, her stillness is reminiscent of her "zen-like" predecessor Roy Orbison. After a few bars of singing, though, it's obvious her internal composure and self-assurance have never wavered. Though lang in recent years and has said she has no plans to return to music, fans can still hope that she'll once again perform.

In a 2019 article for *The Guardian*, lang said, "I grew up with the adage that there is a wealth of purpose in being mysterious . . . and I feel like I haven't had the chance to be mysterious. My sexuality . . . was so much out in the open, and has been for many years. I feel exhausted by being exposed."[5] After a career that spanned nearly four decades, lang, now sixty, prefers to stay out of the spotlight.

At this point, it's fitting to remember that the "Constant Craving" music video, which won an MTV Video Music Award, was inspired by the famous Samuel Beckett play, *Waiting for Godot.* Ironically, trying to get an interview with lang while writing this book has been a bit like *Waiting for Godot.* Despite my numerous attempts to interview lang, I only heard crickets.

Beckett once said of the multiple interpretations of his cryptic play, "Why [do] people have to complicate a thing

---

[5]Hanra, Hanna. "'I Feel Exhausted by Being Exposed': kd lang on Being a Lesbian Icon." *The Guardian.* July 11, 2019.

so simple I can't make out."[6] This quote could have easily been spoken by lang as well. "Maybe . . ." as she sang in her hit "Constant Craving," ". . . a great magnet pulls all souls towards truth . . ." and lang's truth, already stated thirty years post-*Ingénue*, is rightfully enjoying her privacy.

Still, I imagine k.d. like a lesbian folk hero. I picture her a little like Johnny Appleseed in *Angel with a Lariat*-era garb, prancing around a field, dropping seeds from a burlap sack down to the Earth. From those seeds, I imagine a big tree with all these branches: Emily Sailers and Amy Ray of the Indigo Girls, Melissa Etheridge, Melissa Ferrick, Ani DiFranco queer-leaning Riot Grrrl bands like Sleater-Kinney, Le Tigre, Beth Ditto of the Gossip, twin sisters and fellow Canadians, Tegan and Sara Quin, Angel Olsen, King Princess, the amazing Australian rocker Courtney Barnett, and now the contemporary queen of lesbian folk-rock Brandi Carlile.[7] Though the styles of all these musicians are vastly different they all share a fearless queerness because lang blazed the trail.

Certainly, many more out lesbian, bisexual, and queer-identified musicians were around before k.d.. Cris Williamson, for example, predates lang as one of the first out lesbian singer-songwriters in the 1970s. Williamson formed Olivia Records, a label for gay women artists, and released fellow lesbian folk singer Meg Christian's debut album, with

[6]SB to Thomas MacGreevy, August 11, 1955 (TCD). Quoted in Knowlson, J., *Damned to Fame: The Life of Samuel Beckett*. London: Bloomsbury, 1996, 416.

[7]I am omitting countless others who are rumored to be queer, but are not publicly out.

a great gay title, *I Know You Know* (1974), and the second, Williamson's classic *The Changer and the Change* (1975).[8]

In the 1970s, Dusty Springfield, who influenced lang, came out as bisexual, saying, "I know that I'm as perfectly capable of being swayed by a girl as by a boy."[9]

Ray and Saliers of the Indigo Girls, as *Q Voice News* reported, have discussed difficulties they faced with "internalized homophobia" while being closeted. They admit they were not consciously aware their sexuality would be part of history, but Saliers states that "lang and Melissa Etheridge . . . You sort of see them as comrades . . . women in solidarity."[10]

Many other artists are shaping the future, too, with their own acknowledgments. The stunning Janelle Monáe, whose conceptual albums have drawn comparisons to David Bowie's *The Rise and Fall of Ziggy Stardust and the Spiders From Mars*, came out as nonbinary in 2022. Monáe discussed this on Season 5 of *Red Table Talk*, an intergenerational talk show hosted by Jada Pinkett Smith. "I'm nonbinary, so I just don't see myself as a woman, solely," Monáe admitted. "I feel like God is so much bigger than the 'he' or the 'she.' . . . But I will always, always stand with women. I will always stand

---

[8]"Cris Williamson Biography." *AllMusic.* https://www.allmusic.com/artist/cris-williamson-mn0000133456/biography.

[9]Springfield as qtd. in Levine. "How Dusty Springfield Made a Remarkable Comeback." *BBC.* June 30, 2020. https://www.bbc.com/culture/article/20200630-how-dusty-springfield-made-a-remarkable-comeback.

[10]Gilchrist, Tracy. "Indigo Girls Discuss Their Musical History, Lesbian Roots of 'Women's Music.'" *Q Voice News.* September 19, 2021.

with Black women. But I just see everything I am. Beyond the binary."[11]

In Clarissa Pinkola Estés classic *Women Who Run with the Wolves* (1992), she writes:

> For some . . . they seek out the lost people and things in their lives. They take back their voices and write. They rest. They make some corner of the world their own. They execute immense or intense decisions. They do something that leaves footprints.[12]

In this book, I've been able to take back my voice and write. With *Ingénue*, lang did too. She made "some corner of the world [her] own" reclaiming her identity from her former "cowpunk" beginnings to redefining herself through *Ingénue*. When homophobia lurked around every corner, the impact that lang's coming out had at the time of *Ingénue*'s release was pivotal.

lang's voice, as a singer, musician, writer, and activist, is a model for all of us who also seek to share our stories and who are brave enough to relive pivotal moments from our lives that shaped our identities. lang, as Estés describes, left footprints—so, it's no wonder she performs barefoot.

[11]Monáe as qtd. in Street. Street, Mikelle. "Janelle Monae Comes Out as Non-Binary: I am Everything." *The Advocate*. April 2022. https://www.advocate.com/people/2022/4/21/janelle-monae-comes-out-nonbinary-i-am-everything.

[12]Estés, Clarissa Pinkola. *Women Who Run with the Wolves: Myths and Stories of the Wild Woman Archetype*. New York: Ballentine, 1992.

Works Cited

"60 Minutes Australia: Craving More (2017)." *YouTube*, uploaded by 60 Minutes Australia. March 3, 17. https://www.youtube .com/watch?v=03VU0rGeHXI.

Arrow, Michelle. "'Suburban Living Did Turn Women into Robots': Why Feminist Horror Novel *The Stepford Wives* Is Still Relevant 50 Years On." *The Conversation.* July 25, 2022. https:// theconversation.com/suburban-living-did-turn-women-into -robots-why-feminist-horror-novel-the-stepford-wives-is-still -relevant-50-years-on-186633.

Barker, Hugh and Yuval Taylor. *Faking It: The Quest for Authenticity in Popular Music.* New York: Norton, 2007, 237.

Beckett, Samuel as qtd. in Knowlson. *Damned to Fame: The Life of Samuel Beckett.* London: Bloomsbury, 1996, 416.

Bennetts, Leslie. "k.d. lang Cuts It Close." *Vanity Fair.* August 1, 1993. https://www.vanityfair.com/style/1993/08/kd-lang-cover -story.

Bireley, Nesbitt. *Pulse!.* April 1992.

Burton, Gary. "Jazz Vibraphonist Gary Burton." *Fresh Air*, hosted by Terry Gross. *NPR.* January 5, 1994. https://freshairarchive .org/guests/gary-burton.

"The Captain's Wife." *Hacks*, created by Lucia Aniello, Paul W. Downs, and Jen Statsky, season 2, episode 4, Paulilu Productions, 2022.

Clarke, Daniel. Personal Interview. Conducted by the author. July 7, 2022.

"Cole Porter in the Age of AIDS: The 25th Anniversary of 'Red Hot + Blue.'" *PopMatters*. November 19, 2015. https://www.popmatters.com/cole-porter-in-the-age-of-aids-the-25th-anniversary-of-red-hot-blue-2495469079.html.

Contreras, Felix. "Canciones De Amor: Boleros for Your Lover." *NPR*, National Public Radio. February 14, 2008. https://www.npr.org/2008/02/14/19023782/canciones-de-amor-boleros-for-your-lover.

"A Conversation with Cindy Crawford: Clip 4 (On iconic K.D. Lang Vanity Fair cover shoot)." *YouTube*, uploaded by Commonwealth Club of California. December 18, 2015. https://www.youtube.com/watch?v=b6BJmdClJ4k.

"Cris Williamson Biography." *AllMusic*. https://www.allmusic.com/artist/cris-williamson-mn0000133456/biography.

Cromelin, Richard. "POP MUSIC: For k.d. Lang it's Bye-Bye, Patsy – Hello, *Ingénue*." *Los Angeles Times*. August 2, 1992. https://www.latimes.com/archives/la-xpm-1992-08-02-ca-5557-story.html.

"David Piltch." *The Canadian Encyclopedia*. May 9, 2007. https://www.thecanadianencyclopedia.ca/en/article/david-piltch-emc.

Elliott, Robin. "Performing k.d. lang." *Canadian Woman Studies*, vol. 24, no. 2–3, Winter–Spring 2005, 160+.

Eltringham, Fred. Personal Interview. Conducted by the author. June 30, 2022.

Estés, Clarissa Pinkola. *Women Who Run with the Wolves: Myths and Stories of the Wild Woman Archetype*. New York: Ballentine, 1992.

"Flashback: k.d. lang Comes out on the Cover of the Advocate Magazine, June 16, 1992." *IN Magazine*, Elevate Media Group Inc. June 16, 2022. https://inmagazine.ca.

Frith, Simon. *Performing Rites: On the Value of Popular Music.* Cambridge, MA: Harvard University Press, 1998.

"George Harrison Guilty of Plagiarizing, Subconsciously, a '62 Tune for a '70 Hit." *The New York Times.* September 8, 1976.

Gilchrist, Tracy. "Indigo Girls Discuss Their Musical History, Lesbian Roots of 'Women's Music.'" *Q Voice News.* September 19, 2021.

Goldin-Perschbacher, Shana. *Queer Country.* Champaign, IL: University of Illinois Press, 2022.

"Great Performances: k.d. lang—Landmarks Live in Concert." *PBS.* December 14, 2018. https://www.pbs.org/wnet/gperf/k-d -lang-landmarks-live-in-concert-a-great-performances-special -about/9068/.

Hanra, Hanna. "'I Feel Exhausted by Being Exposed': kd lang on Being a Lesbian Icon." *The Guardian.* July 11, 2019.

Hilton, Robin. "k.d. lang Reflects on 25 Years of Ingénue." *NPR.* July 13, 2017.

Holden, Stephen. "POP VIEW; Why Cole Porter Prevails—Be It Pop, Rock, or Even Rap." *New York Times.* October 21, 1990. https://www.nytimes.com/1990/10/21/arts/pop-view-why-cole -porter-prevails-be-it-pop-rock-or-even-rap.html.

Jackson, Blair. "Classic Track: 'Constant Craving,' k.d. Lang." *Mix Magazine Online.* August 1, 2013.

Joyce, Mike. "Etheridge: Out and About." *The Washington Post.* July 6, 1994. https://www.washingtonpost.com/archive/lifestyle /1994/07/06/etheridge-out-and-about/9e02cbb4-b7da-4599 -82fd-a3fe398a6787.

Joyce, Mike. "K.D. Lang." *The Washington Post.* July 13, 1992. https://www.washingtonpost.com/archive/lifestyle/1992/07/13/ kd-lang/efd73f5b-07da-4c73-9603-2a0e560c2138/.

"k.d. lang Interview—Barbara Walters 1993." *YouTube,* uploaded by The lang Channel. April 14, 2013. https://www.youtube.com /watch?v=wivERtlHPYA.

"k.d. lang Interview on Sexuality Patsy Cline and Roy Orbison—
    Later with Bob Costas 4/28/92." *YouTube*, uploaded by
    clevelandlivemusic. February 16, 2021. https://www.youtube
    .com/watch?v=1LW4p7GLof8.

"K.D. Lang Looks Back at Her Iconic Junos Win for most Promising
    Female | Junos 50th." *YouTube*, uploaded by *CBC Music*. https://
    www.youtube.com/watch?v=wynWxugM8Bs&t=45s.

"k.d. lang—MTV Music Awards 1993." *YouTube*, uploaded by The
    lang Channel. June 1, 2013. https://www.youtube.com/watch?v
    =RUDXyavRYcw.

"K.D. Lang, Outside Myself and Season of Hollow Soul." *YouTube*,
    uploaded by rocky storm. n.d. https://www.youtube.com/watch
    ?v=_DTEN858KKM.

"k.d. lang Profile and Interview on Face to Face with Connie
    Chung 1990, pt. 1 of 2." *YouTube*, uploaded by Abstorch. n.d.
    https://www.youtube.com/watch?v=IJFMcTa1XnA.

"k.d. lang Thinks She's a 1 Hit Wonder." *YouTube*, uploaded by Q
    on CBC. February 27, 2017. https://www.youtube.com/watch?v
    =SuKfPqwitKk.

"kdlanginterview." *YouTube*, uploaded by Eddie Sams. August 17,
    2022. https://www.youtube.com/watch?v=C5jw5ReluVw.

Kinser, Jeremy. "Arsenio Hall Explains His Notorious On-Air
    Argument with Gay Rights Activists." *Queerty*. August 7, 2013.
    https://www.queerty.com/arsenio-hall-explains-his-notorious
    -on-air-argument-with-gay-rights-activists-20130807.

Kohanov, Linda. "Chanteuse Extraordinaire: k.d. lang." *Pulse!*.
    April 1992, 73–7.

lang, k.d. "The Immortals—Greatest Artists of All Time: 37 - Roy
    Orbison." *Rolling Stone*, no. 946. April 15, 2004.

lang, k.d. as qtd. in Mockus. "Queer Thoughts: On Country
    Music and k.d. lang." *Queering the Pitch*, ed. by Philip Brett,
    Elizabeth Wood, and Gary C. Thomas. New York: Routledge,
    1994, 353.

lang, k.d. as qtd. in Simpson. "kd lang and Ben Mink: How
    We Made 'Constant Craving.'" *The Guardian*. https://www
    .theguardian.com/music/2017/sep/26/kd-lang-ben-mink-how
    -we-made-constant-craving.

lang, k.d. as qtd. in Udovitch. "k.d. lang." *Rolling Stone*. August 5,
    1993, 55–7.

lang, k.d. [kdlang]. *Twitter*. November 24, 2016. https://twitter.com
    /kdlang/status/801848405794267136?lang=en.

Levine, Nick. "How Dusty Springfield Made a Remarkable
    Comeback." *BBC*. June 30, 2020. https://www.bbc.com/culture
    /article/20200630-how-dusty-springfield-made-a-remarkable
    -comeback.

"Madonna's Truth or Dare Premiere Party - MTV Special -
    1991 - Part 01." *YouTube*, uploaded by RetroSpectoVideos.
    February 25, 2013. https://www.youtube.com/watch?v=ma
    _T_javZFs.

Martin, Biddy. "Lesbian Identity and Autobiographical
    Difference(s)." *The Lesbian and Gay Studies Reader*, ed. by
    Henry Abelove, et al. New York: Routledge, 1993, 274–93.

McNaney, Joanna. *The Life Cycle Library*. M.F.A. Thesis, Pacific
    Lutheran University, 2008.

McNaney, Joanna. *Split*. M.A. Thesis, State University of New York,
    College at Brockport, 2004.

"Melissa Ethridge & KD Lang - You Can Sleep - The Beat Goes
    On - 1994." *YouTube*, uploaded by LIFEbeat. n.d. https://www
    .youtube.com/watch?v=vE4nij3AZso.

Mink, Ben. Personal Interview. Conducted by the author.
    December 3, 2021.

Mink, Ben. as qtd. in Jackson. "Classic Track: 'Constant Craving,'
    k.d. Lang." *Mix Magazine Online*. August 1, 2013.

"Miss Chatelaine / Constant Craving & Interview - 1993." *YouTube*,
    uploaded by The Lang Channel. n.d. https://www.youtube.com/
    watch?v=Qqo6xaiFky8.

Mockus, Martha. "Queer Thoughts: On Country Music and k.d. lang." *Queering the Pitch*, ed. by Philip Brett, Elizabeth Wood, and Gary C. Thomas. New York: Routledge, 1994, 349.

Monae as qtd. in Street. "Janelle Monae Comes Out as Non-Binary: I am Everything." *The Advocate*. April 2022. https:// www.advocate.com/people/2022/4/21/janelle-monae-comes -out-nonbinary-i-am-everything.

Newman, Melinda. "Grammy Win Propels lang to Platinum Status." *Billboard*, vol. 105, no. 12, March 20, 1993.

Pareles, Jon. "CABARET: K.D. LANG, COUNTRY." *The New York Times*, May 10, 1987. https://www.nytimes.com/1987/05/10/ arts/cabaret-kd-lang-country.html.

Penny as qtd. in Jackson. "Classic Track: 'Constant Craving,' k.d. Lang." *Mix Magazine Online*. August 1, 2013. https://www .mixonline.com/recording/classic-track-constant-craving-kd -lang-366433.

Philby, Charlotte. "My Secret Life: KD Lang." *The Independent*. July 25, 2009. https://www.independent.co.uk/news/people/profiles/ my-secret-life-kd-lang-1757220.html.

Piltch, David. "Re: Form Submission—Inquiries." Received by Joanna McNaney Stein. January 24, 2023. Email Interview.

"Roy Orbison." *Memphis Music Hall of Fame*. https://memphismusi challoffame.com/inductee/royorbison/.

Sacks, Oliver. *Musicophilia*. Vintage Books, 2007, 325.

Schlessinger as qtd. in Ladd. "StopDrLaura.com." *Salon*. March 1, 2000. https://www.salon.com/2000/03/01/drlaura_2/.

Shewey, Don. "Madonna: The X-Rated Interview." *The Advocate*. May 7, 1991.

Simpson, Dave. "kd lang and Ben Mink: How We Made 'Constant Craving.'" *The Guardian*. https://www.theguardian.com/music /2017/sep/26/kd-lang-ben-mink-how-we-made-constant -craving.

WORKS CITED

"Singer k.d. lang on 'letting your freak flag fly.'" *CBC News*. April 22, 2013.

Snapes, Laura. "k.d. lang: Ingénue." *Pitchfork*. September 8, 2019. https://pitchfork.com/reviews/albums/kd-lang-Ingénue/.

Spirit Studios and Christopher Sweeney. "K.d. lang Part 1." *Homo Sapiens*, Spotify. August 2021.

Springfield as qtd. in Levine. "How Dusty Springfield Made a Remarkable Comeback." *BBC*. June 30, 2020. https://www.bbc.com/culture/article/20200630-how-dusty-springfield-made-a-remarkable-comeback.

Street, Mikelle. "Janelle Monae Comes Out as Non-Binary: I am Everything." *The Advocate*. April 2022. https://www.advocate.com/people/2022/4/21/janelle-monae-comes-out-nonbinary-i-am-everything.

Styron, William as qtd. in Sacks. *Musicophilia*. Vintage Books, 2007, 325.

Toureille, Claire. "'k.d. lang Hints Madonna Relationship Was a Showmance to Help 'Sell Records.'" *Daily Mail Online*. Associated Newspapers, June 16, 2019. https://www.dailymail.co.uk/ushome/index.html.

"Turn Me Round and 3 Cigarettes k.d. lang Back on Carson Show a Week Later!" *YouTube*, uploaded by Declan John. n.d. https://www.youtube.com/watch?v=BD_n6ju9iRA.

Udovitch, Mim. "k.d. lang." *Rolling Stone*. August 5, 1993, 55–7.

Veirs, Laura. Personal Interview. Conducted by the author. June 6, 2022.

Wanagas as qtd. in Newman. "Grammy Win Propels lang to Platinum Status." *Billboard*, vol. 105, no. 12, March 20, 1993.

"Webster! Interview with K.D. lang." *YouTube*, uploaded by Royal BC Museum. October 24, 2014. https://www.youtube.com/watch?v=S_7ExsNi9pw.

Whalen, Tracy. "Engendering Charisma: k.d. lang and the Comic Frame." *Intertexts*, vol. 18, no. 1, Spring 2014, 9+.

Wilsey, Sean. "The Things They Buried." Rev. of *Fun Home*, by Alison Bechdel. *New York Times Book Review*. June 18, 2006, 9.

Wood, Elizabeth. "Sapphonics." *Queering the Pitch*, ed. by Philip Brett, Elizabeth Wood, and Gary C. Thomas. New York: Routledge, 1994, 51.

Also Available in the Series

ALSO AVAILABLE IN THE SERIES